THE ETHICAL
AFTERMATH OF
AUTOMATION

EDITED BY FRANCIS X. QUINN, S.J.

THE ETHICAL

AFTERMATH OF

AUTOMATION

THE NEWMAN PRESS • WESTMINSTER, MARYLAND

1962

301.243
Q7

Imprimi potest: R. P. GULIELMUS F. MALONEY, S.J.
    Vice-Praepositus Provincialis
    Provinciae Marylandiae

    October 23, 1961

Nihil obstat: EDWARD A. CERNY, S.S., S.T.D.

Imprimatur: LAWRENCE J. SHEHAN, D.D.

    March 30, 1962

"It is *therefore an exigency of social justice that such application be made in such a way that the immediate negative results of automation should not be borne exclusively by the workers or by certain groups of workers. Rather should such negative results weigh equally, or even more heavily, upon the investors of capital and, when opportune, even upon all the members of the political community, since all, in the final analysis, benefit by such changes of automation. This can the more surely be obtained when the workers, through their unions and organizations, are present and have a voice in the implementation of processes of automation.*"

A LETTER OF HIS EMINENCE

AMLETO GIOVANNI CARDINAL CICOGNANI,
Papal Secretary of State

TO ARCHBISHOP BERRY OF HALIFAX

July 27th, 1961

CONTENTS

INTRODUCTION AND PREFACE   3
Francis X. Quinn, S.J.

1. HUMAN ASPECTS OF AUTOMATION   7
Daniel L. Shields, Jr.

2. COLLECTIVE BARGAINING AND AUTOMATION   19
Rev. Benjamin L. Masse, S.J.

3. AUTOMATION AND MANPOWER IN THE 1960s   27
Seymour L. Wolfbein

4. ETHICS AND ECONOMIC SECURITY   37
Rev. Dennis J. Comey, S.J.

5. LABOR AND AUTOMATION   49
Abraham Weiss

6. ETHICS, ECONOMICS, AND CHRONIC UNEMPLOY-
MENT IN THE MIDST OF AUTOMATED ABUN-
DANCE   65
Rev. William J. Byron, S.J.

7. AUTOMATION AND THE OLDER WORKER   87
James C. O'Brien

8. AUTOMATION AND MANAGEMENT DECISIONS   103
Rev. Thomas M. Garrett, S.J.

9. AUTOMATION AND THE WELFARE OF THE
COUNTRY   113
Joseph D. Keenan

10. MANY FACETS OF THE PROBLEM   127
John O'Neil

vii

11. THE PROMOTION OF ETHICS BY AUTOMATION   143
George M. Muschamp

12. AUTOMATION-AGE APOSTLES
Contemplativus in Actione   153
Rev. Thomas P. Gavigan, S.J.

13. AUTOMATION-AGE APOSTLES
Secular Institutes   163
Dr. John J. O'Connor

14. AUTOMATION IN THE LIFE OF A CATHOLIC   175
Rev. Gustave Weigel, S.J.

15. A CONSERVATIVE VIEWS AUTOMATION   187
U. S. Senator Barry M. Goldwater

16. CULTURAL DIMENSIONS OF THE NEW LEISURE   199
Rev. W. Norris Clarke, S.J.

17. POLITICAL, SOCIAL, AND ECONOMIC IMPLICATIONS
OF AUTOMATION   213
U. S. Senator Eugene J. McCarthy

18. THE ETHICAL AFTERMATH OF AUTOMATION   229
Rt. Rev. George G. Higgins

APPENDIX
THE BENEFITS AND PROBLEMS INCIDENT TO
AUTOMATION AND OTHER TECHNOLOGICAL
ADVANCES   241
President's Advisory Committee on Labor-Management, Arthur J. Goldberg, Chairman
COMMENTS BY ARTHUR F. BURNS   253
COMMENTS BY HENRY FORD II   256

A SELECTED BIBLIOGRAPHY ON AUTOMATION   261
Francis X. Quinn, S.J.

INDEX   267

THE ETHICAL
AFTERMATH OF
AUTOMATION

INTRODUCTION
AND PREFACE

by FRANCIS X. QUINN, S.J., *Woodstock College*

ONE FACT APPARENT to the most casual observer of the industrial scene is that automation, though itself no newcomer to the competitive marketplace, is gaining a stronger foothold and a wider degree of usefulness as science and technology make consistently rapid progress. The problems which this fact creates are legion. The aftermath of automation involves expanding industry and the vitalization of various crafts. It induces change in the very environment of work. By changing the ratio between blue and white collar workers. it affects the character of the work force and the jurisdiction of unions themselves. How do we decide who shall bear the cost of technological change and who shall receive the major benefits of it? How do we create an atmosphere which accepts adaptation as a necessary pattern in labor-management relations? The complex ethical questions seem to multiply. Can the economy absorb the displaced skilled as well as the unskilled without great delay? Will we provide for older workers and for depressed areas? What is the role of collective bargaining? How will the worker use increased leisure?

These questions and their many derivatives were the object of discussions held at Woodstock College, Woodstock,

3

Maryland, from August 6th to 11th, 1961. Twenty-seven experts on automation from government, industry, education, labor, and management addressed their observations to students of Woodstock and their invited guests. The eighteen chapters of this book represent eighteen position papers presented by experts to other experts and students. The Appendix contains The Report on Automation by the President's Advisory Committee on Labor-Management and a selected bibliography on automation.

These experts unanimously agree that in the long run automation is the key to some of labor's chief goals: the shorter week, higher wages and better working conditions. Potential victims of automation, however, must be forgiven if they do not derive much comfort from the thought that future generations will consider their sufferings as the necessary price to be paid for the sake of the high standard of living which those generations will enjoy. The experts, therefore, offer both long and short range proposals to meet the aftermath which is with us.

But why should priests and students for the priesthood concern themselves with automation or its effects? As we were preparing this seminar, an editorial voice from *Fortune* magazine rang in our ears: "Business has become so complex that many of its ramifications have got beyond the understanding of our moral instructors, the clergy, and the moral understanding of businessmen themselves. There is a gray area where there are no written rules of conduct" (*Fortune,* March, 1961, p. 104).

Much of the aftermath of automation concerns rights and obligations, how man ought to live at home, at rest, at recreation. Rights can only be secured where duties are performed and where virtue flourishes between man and man. Seen thus, many of the issues of the aftermath of automation are fundamentally ethical and moral issues.

The theologians, philosophers, economists, sociologists,

4

educators and legislators, experts lay and cleric, whose ideas you will read in these pages, helped us to open the door on a "gray area." The seminar was intended to be an introduction to the complexities of automation, a presentation of fact and viewpoint and an invitation for discussion of an urgent issue. This it has accomplished. In that same spirit it is now offered in print.

If our increased leisure is to mean something more than just another day when we can sleep late, all of us will need to develop our understanding, our interests, ourselves. In the aftermath of automation, it will be our ability to think, to judge, and to understand which will elevate us above the automated. Machines are only machines; it is up to men to decide how to use them ethically.

Neither the seminar nor this book would have been possible without the encouragement and help of the men of Woodstock. The editor owes a very special debt to Rev. Joseph M. Hamernick, S.J., & Mr. Edward Woods, Washington Correspondent of the *St. Louis Post-Dispatch* for their invaluable advice and assistance.

CHAPTER 1

HUMAN ASPECTS
OF AUTOMATION

by DANIEL L. SHIELDS, JR., *Industrial Psychologist, Professor of Automation, St. Joseph's College, Institute of Industrial Relations*

Introduction

THE PURPOSE of this portion of the seminar, as I understand it, is to discuss the phenomenon of automation with a view to developing a basic concept of what automation is and to translate this concept into some meaningful, human term. In attempting this, we shall, due to the complexity of the problem and considerations of time, limit the discussion to automation as it affects the industrial scene, and forego any consideration of the overall cultural impact of automation. The discussion will start with a brief examination of what automation is, continue with a cursory inspection of the problem through the eyes of man as a manager and as a laborer, and conclude with a more detailed examination of the implications of automation for man as a man.

What is Automation?

Automation means many things to many people. In attempting to develop a working concept, we shall consider

7

automation in terms of some accepted definitions, its historical perspective and the techniques that underlie automation.

Automation has been defined as "the supplementing of man's senses and his brain power by devices which collect and process information, transmit it to the point needed, and there either control machines or present the information to humans for their use." [1]

It has also been defined as "the substitution of mechanical, pneumatic, hydraulic, electrical or electronic devices for the human organs of observation, decision and effort, so as to increase productivity, control quality, and reduce cost." [2]

Automation has at its heart the basic concept of cybernetics. This is the field of control or communication theory (in machines or animals). The name is derived from the Greek word for steersman and was selected for its connotation of the regulated feedback involved in steering a ship. This use of feedback information to regulate and thereby integrate a complex process is one of the key concepts underlying automation. For just as the swinging arc of the bow, the curve of the wake, and the changing compass reading all feed back information on the ship's turning motion through the helmsman's eye to his hand on the wheel, so do modern feedback devices monitor the performance of work and provide electrical signals to equipment controls in order to regulate the manufacturing process. Thus is information conveyed by other than the spoken or written word.

Historically, automation is a modern extension of the age-old process of technological evolution wherein gifted designers have given us machines which substitute for, or supplement, man's capabilities. In place of man's muscle we have learned to use steam, electricity, and the atom; in place of man's muscle we have learned to use the lever, the wheel, the press and the forge; and to supplement man's senses, judgment, and memory we have learned to use such devices as the thermometer, the scale, the thermostat, and the computer. More specifically, automation has been called a second industrial revolution providing substitutes for man's senses and brain power as the first industrial revolution provided substitutes for his muscles. Among its antecedents have been the automated flour mill of Evans in Philadelphia (1784), where wheat was made into flour with no human intervention other than to furnish the grain and bag the flour. It is descended from Jacquard's looms (1801), which used punched holes in paper tapes to regulate the weaving process.

But it is what is new about automation that interests us. And this is the fact that automation is a concept that results in a generalized technological improvement that applies to all industries, rather than just a few; and that it is riding on the crest of a tidal wave of research breakthroughs.

Underlying the new "technology" are three fundamental techniques, namely, integration, feedback, and computer technology. Integration links conventionally separate manufacturing operations into a line of continuous automatic production by mechanizing the handling of the materials of production. Feedback control devices allow individual manufacturing operations to be performed without individual human control. These devices usually include a capacity for checking and correcting the performance of work. Computer technology speeds up the processing of information by providing the capability to record, to store and to perform mathematical operations on data. The modern home oil heating system serves as an everyday, though somewhat forced, illustration of these three techniques working together. Thus, the transfer of fuel oil to the combustion chamber may be taken to repre-

9

sent integration; the regulation of the heating process by the thermostat, which senses the difference between a desired state of warmth and the actual state and controls the heating process in accordance with this difference, may be taken to represent feedback; and the oil company's calculation of degree days as related to fuel requirements may be taken to represent computer technology. What this means in terms of human labor not needed to feed fuel to the furnace, or to regulate the draft, or to order fuel, is apparent. What this means as a simple illustration of cybernetics at work—with information being generated by the physics of the thermometer transmitted by the electricity of the thermostat and acted upon by electronics of the computer—is truly striking. Automation offers similar possibilities in regard to industry's material handlers, machine operators, supervisors, and planners.

Thus far, then, automation has been considered in terms of some definitions, its origin and the techniques that underlie it. Now, what about the human implications of this? Here the best point of departure is the people who are most directly affected by automation, namely, the managers and the laborers themselves. Consider management first.

Management's Viewpoint

And from management's point of view . . .

Automation is evolutionary in nature; its progress is based upon extensive, time-consuming research and development efforts in the areas of materials development and product design, as well as in the areas of manufacturing, management, and distribution techniques.

Automation represents an opportunity to increase

productivity, decrease cost, increase purchasing power and improve working conditions.

Automation is necessary to . . .

—get the greatest return in productivity for every dollar of capital invested in equipment. This is especially critical during an inflationary period when the tendency and ability to save money for investment purposes decreases.

—continue to raise the standard of living.

—release productive capacity for products just coming into being.

—allow the potential worker to enter the labor force later in life, to leave it earlier, and to work less hours all the while he is a member of the working force.

—compete in the world's markets, especially if wages are to continue to increase.

Management concedes that certainly there are some risks involved. But at the level of the individual company the manager asks, "If I don't automate and reduce my work force 20 per cent, all of my workers stand to lose their jobs as my competitors become more efficient. And isn't management responsible to the stockholders and the public, as well as to employees?" And, finally, management maintains that automation will . . .

—stimulate the economy, for as productivity increases, costs decrease, prices decrease, sales increase, and employment increases.

—stabilize the economy, because you plan carefully in terms of anticipated product demand before you invest heavily in capital equipment.

11

—create employment as new industries become possible; for example, the atomic energy industry; as the manufacture of automated equipment itself increases in volume; and as the higher standard of living creates more demand for service occupations.

And what is labor's opinion concerning all this?

Labor's Viewpoint

From Labor's point of view . . .

Automation is by nature a continuation of technological evolution, but at a rapidly accelerating pace which is aided by the sustained high research and development effort necessitated in the military area because of the cold war.

Automation represents an opportunity to eliminate dangerous and monotonous jobs, to upgrade the overall skill level of labor, to decrease costs and thus either reduce prices or increase wages, and to create new industries and products which in turn create new job opportunities.

Automation is a problem. It is a problem of balancing with increased consuming power the yearly increases in productivity that flow from three sources. The first is better (and in many cases better means automated) equipment. The second is a work force with one more year's experience. The third is the net gain in working force size. (To gain some idea of the seriousness of this problem consider the following facts. Each year more people enter the labor force than there are new jobs. During the period 1960-1970, 14,000,000 people will join the ranks of the labor force. This represents an average annual increase of 1,400,000 people *vs.* an average annual increase of 838,000 during the period 1950-1960. During the period 1947-1960, the total output of the U. S. economy increased 56 per cent, while employment increased 11 per cent and the average weekly hours worked declined 7 per cent.[3] To achieve and maintain this desired balance between productivity and consumption, in light of facts such as we have just outlined, labor proposes a program that calls for:

—a guaranteed annual wage as a means of providing the income equivalent of guaranteed employment, and of regulating the timing and location of technological innovation by minimizing at least the initial savings that accrue from displacing labor with machines.

—higher pay for automated jobs, since the skill of the worker is needed to unleash the full potential of the new machinery, and since the worker becomes responsible for a greater volume of production and for a more valuable piece of capital equipment.

—shorter term, more easily amended contracts to allow labor to adjust to a rapidly changing situation.

—a reduction in the working life span brought about by starting to work later in life and retiring earlier through a higher standard of living, and by shortening the work week and lengthening vacation periods.

—government aid in such forms as higher minimum wages, increased unemployment compensation, increased social security, favorable taxes, increased public works, and aid to low income families.

And behind this more sophisticated problem there is the more basic, personal problem. What about displace-

13

ment: displacement of the worker directly replaced by the machine: displacement of the competitors' employees, let go as the competition loses part of his share of the market to the better automated company. Here the program proposes:

—retraining to adapt to new jobs.

—relocation to areas of labor shortage.

—retirement of older employees to create openings.

And, underlying all this there is the inevitable question, "Who is going to pay for this?" and "Who is going to pay for the equity lost through displacement—the seniority, status, insurance pension, and vacations built up over a long association with a particular company?"

These are the things labor sees in automation.

Man As Man

The foregoing has been offered to provide a quick glimpse into the minds of managers and laborers as they ponder the problem of automation. There is a deeper human problem however. For before all else, before being managers or laborers, these are men—human beings. What does automation mean for man, as man?

Niall Brennan in his book, *The Making of a Moron*,[4] develops a very interesting thesis concerning industrial society. His point is that "modern" industry, which devours so much of the life span of the average individual, does not encourage and in many instances does not allow workers at all levels to apply their full, human capabilities. (This is seen most vividly in the wide-spread complete separation of the planning and doing functions in so many enterprises.) The consequence of this is that these capabilities atrophy through disuse, and eventually, as is the case with the moron, the individual does not enjoy the full exercise of his faculties.

A much broader and deeper development of this basic concept of the relation of industrial society to human nature derives from the social encyclicals, *Rerum Novarum* and *Quadragesimo Anno,* whence evolve such concepts of the ideal social order as the following:

> The social order is organic, being composed of living human beings rather than cogs, and in it, work is social and involves the mind and will in seeking a common good.

> The ultimate purpose of the social order is to develop as fully as possible every human person, that is, to develop the greatest capacity for happiness by developing the intellect and will.

> The economic purpose is to develop production and to insure just distribution, thereby supplying the means to maintain and develop the human personality.

> The basic principle is that man is a human being with inherent dignity and a son of God by reason of adoption and grace.

> It operates by the principle of subsidiarity; that is, it diffuses responsibility as widely as possible, thus developing both the intellect and will.

Automation can, of course, be a help or a hindrance in attaining this ideal; and, on this basis, we see the full import of automation as a human problem.

> With regard to the economic purpose of the social order, automation obviously increases the capacity to produce things. But is it a true increase of productivity in the national economy? In the words of Pius XII, automation

... obviously increases productive capacity fantastically. Does it also, however, increase the true productivity of the national economy? By this we mean the lasting and true attainment of conditions which make possible the material and human well-being of all members of the population so that all who contribute directly to the national economy through their work, their land or capital, will earn an income comparable to their contribution. Furthermore, such national economic productivity should make it possible to overcome social tensions more easily.[5]

With regard to the ultimate purpose and basic principle of social order, automation poses both a promise and a threat for the full development of the human personality and the inherent dignity of man. For as technology advances by developing machines that better approximate the capabilities of man, the focus becomes sharper on man's uniquely human capabilities. The result of this sharper focus may be either a renewed respect for what man is, or a heightened disregard for human capability as machines become capable of performing more and more of man's industrial functions. The consequence may be either the creation of a greater number of jobs which release man from drudgery and challenge his highest capabilities, or the creation of a greater number of jobs which demand ever less of human capabilities as the machine assumes ever more "responsibility."

With regard to the principle of subsidiarity, or the diffusion of responsibility, automation, as a challenge, offers tremendous arenas for the exercise of intellect and will. How far the responsibility for answering this challenge is diffused will be determined by the degree to which the individual worker or manager relies on himself, his union or his company, his international or his industry, or his government.

And it is this aspect of automation, as it touches on the nature of the individual and the nature of the society in which he lives, that is most significant.

16

Conclusion

Thus far we have considered what automation is; we have backed off and looked at it through the eyes of management and labor, and we have examined it as a problem with fundamental implications for human beings. In conclusion then, we can note that, as a human problem, automation is essentially a philosophical problem. For while the sociologist, the psychologist, the engineer and the economist can all study automation, and while, hopefully, they can exchange information to sharpen their own conclusions against the findings of other disciplines, they must always qualify their conclusions with "sociologically speaking," "psychologically speaking," "technically speaking" or "economically speaking." And it remains for the philosopher, with his charter to examine all things in light of ultimate causes—with his concern for the nature of things and for the relationships deriving therefrom—to assign value and order to the findings of the various social and natural sciences. Consequently, I have welcomed the opportunity to discuss the problem of automation with this particular group of scholastic philosophers, and I hope you will find the talk of some benefit in orienting a complex problem to the searching analysis it will receive this week.

NOTES

1. National Association of Manufacturers, *Calling All Jobs* (November, 1954).
2. First International Automation Exposition, *America* (December, 1954).
3. *U. S. News and World Report* (February, 1961).
4. Niall Brennan, *The Making of a Moron* (New York: Sheed and Ward, 1953).
5. Pope Pius XII, *Address to Christian Association of Italian Workers* (June 7, 1957).

CHAPTER 2

COLLECTIVE BARGAINING AND AUTOMATION

by REV. BENJAMIN L. MASSE, S.J.
Associate Editor of America *Magazine*

I BELIEVE THAT it was Secretary of Labor, Arthur Goldberg, who was the first to talk in terms of a crisis in collective bargaining. Two years ago, at the University of Wisconsin, he spoke of the hardening attitudes of labor and management and their growing estrangement. He noticed this especially in the relationships between unions and employers in the basic industries of the country. Even at that time, he had some notion of bringing labor and management together apart from the bargaining table where the adversary aspect of industrial relations is prominent, and he proposed something like a U.N. assembly in which the leaders of both sides could be brought together to discuss the big issues bedeviling their relationships.

A year later in Chicago, Secretary Goldberg gave another talk at Roosevelt University that was somewhat more specific. He said that we live in an age of technological change and international tension. "Traditional practices," he argued,

which have served us so well and which would continue to do so if we were really at peace must be adapted to a period where our whole way of life is being challenged. Traditional

19

practices which served us so well must be adapted to an age when our industrial society is being transformed by technological advance.

He appealed on that occasion to labor and management to regain that sense of common interest and mutual purpose which animated them during the second World War. Very significantly, he compared our present status to the crisis of World War II, intimating that some similar effort on the part of labor and management was called for today to deal with the situation.

By the time Mr. Goldberg gave the second speech, others had gotten into the act, among them our dear friend and greatly respected authority, Monsignor Higgins. He did not get into it by name exactly, but in July of 1960 he attended a meeting in California, sponsored by the Fund for the Republic, at which a group of leaders of labor and management and other experts discussed the crisis in collective bargaining. On reading over a summary of the conference, I deduced that although the conferees agreed on the existence of a crisis, there was no unanimity on what should be done about it.

One group at the conference was so impressed by the complexities of today's problems that it despaired of any exclusively labor-management approach to them. This group called for a national, coordinated approach in which the federal government would have a substantial role. They recommended the creation in the Executive branch of a council composed of government officials and leaders from management and labor which would thresh out problems too big for the bargaining table and would seek to reach agreements on broad policies.

Another group felt that traditional methods of collective bargaining were not so inadequate that they could not be adapted to the changing times. They conceded that some place had to be made today for public representation in labor-management affairs, but they believed that this could be provided for without involving the government. It was suggested, for instance, that the role of arbitrators might be enlarged so that they could act more creatively and energetically than is now the case, or that labor-management meetings on a regional or industry level be held in which the public would be represented. All the conferees agreed that in any event both labor and management had to abandon some of their cherished positions, and that what was urgently needed was a new spirit of cooperation for the common good.

A friend of mine, Solomon Barkin, who is Research Director of the Textile Workers, wrote an article in *Fortune* magazine, November, 1960, in which he described what he characterized as the low estate of collective bargaining in the United States. He recalled the days when foreign trade unionists flocked to this country after the second World War to see how we did things, and he noticed that European trade unionists were not coming to our shores anymore. He felt that this was because collective bargaining was not functioning so well at the present time. Other voices have been chanting a similar refrain, and all last year the Columbia University Seminar on Labor, which began with a talk by Secretary Goldberg, devoted its resources to a study of the crisis in collective bargaining.

Certain themes recur time and time again as one goes through the literature on the subject. One of these is automation. This process by which machines replace men has gone much faster than anybody thought it would five or six years ago, and now it is very easy to quote startling figures on how production has expanded in, say, manufacturing industry as a whole over a ten-year period, while the labor force engaged has declined. The figures for such

21

industries as the railroads and coal mining are very dramatic, and very frightening. There can be no question about it that a very considerable displacement of workers has occurred by reason of rapid technological advance.

Hardly anybody is against automation. As a matter of fact, nearly everybody is for it because it is a word which has implications of "progress." Predictions of dire consequences from automation usually end with the warning that it must be controlled rather than stopped, and that countermeasures must be taken against its harmful effects. These countermeasures include restrictions on the rate of technological change, retraining programs for displaced workers and relief measures for areas adversely affected. The problem of the displaced worker is especially acute. How do you put him back to work? If you retrain him, what do you retrain him for? And how do you support him and his family during the retraining period? But whatever you do, all these remedial measures are beyond the capacity of labor and management.

Associated with the problem of technological advance are a number of other problems, including the problem of working rules, which has bedeviled industrial relations in the past few years. It was the issue of working rules that caused a breakdown in bargaining on the railroads. At the present time, a presidential commission is engaged in extensive hearings in an effort to reach some sort of an agreement between labor and management on this problem. You may recall that working rules were also a key issue in the great steel strike a year and a half or so ago.

Then, too, there is the whole problem of inflation, which is closely related to the competitive challenge from abroad and the U. S. balance of international payments. Collective bargaining is ill-adapted to cope with these issues, which are a matter of concern to the government and our entire society.

Industry is inclined to say that there is nothing wrong with collective bargaining that cannot be easily cured by destroying the monopoly power of labor, by subjecting labor to the anti-trust acts and by destroying the source of its monopoly power in union security. In other words, by passing right-to-work laws.

To this, the NAM adds that it would be very helpful if votes were required before strikes could be legally called. This powerful organization has the idea that union leaders can order their members to hit the bricks regardless of rank-and-file sentiment, and that strike votes are not actually held today. The NAM feels, furthermore, that the labor-management atmosphere would be much improved if unions were barred from participating in politics.

Some unions are also of the opinion that there is no crisis in industrial relations today, at least not in the terms in which Secretary Goldberg defines it. By and large, the old AFL Building Trades unions are not aware of any special problems in their industries. Neither are the Teamsters, especially now that Jimmy Hoffa has come into his inheritance. In fact, on the labor side, the crisis seems to be exclusively an affair of the former CIO industrial unions, plus the Railroad Brotherhoods and perhaps the Machinists.

Since industry professes to be unaware of any critical change in industrial relations, it has opposed the proposal to get together with labor apart from the bargaining table. The reaction of the Big Two in the auto industry is fairly typical. When former President Eisenhower went to Detroit last October, 1960, to do his best for Mr. Nixon, he interpolated in his speech an exhortation to the UAW and the auto manufacturers to sit down together and discuss the industry's problems. A few days later, Walter Reuther, who knows a good thing when he sees it, wrote

23

letters to Ford and General Motors inviting them, in accordance with the suggestion of the then president of the United States, to sit down and have a little discussion of their common difficulties. The auto magnates turned Mr. Reuther down cold.

Earlier the NAM had made it very clear that it was not interested in a summit meeting, and this circumstance helps to explain why the idea was so long getting off the ground.

In the fall of 1959, President George Meany of the AFL-CIO, who by that time had come to accept Mr. Goldberg's idea, asked President Eisenhower to call a meeting of top labor and management people under the aegis but not the domination of the White House. Apparently this request resulted in a split within the Eisenhower Administration. At any rate, about four months went by before Mr. Eisenhower acted on Mr. Meany's motion; and when he did make his move, he proceeded in such a way that the projected meeting was doomed before it started.

This requires a little explaining.

As I have already said, the NAM was hostile to the summit idea. This was known, of course, to the AFL-CIO. Accordingly, when at a press conference held early in March, 1960, Mr. Meany was asked what the prospect would be if President Eisenhower invited the NAM to represent industry at a summit conference, he replied that in that event nothing would be accomplished. He said that if the conferees were not to waste their time industry should be represented by the heads of companies which dealt with AFL-CIO unions.

To those familiar with these developments, the announcement from the White House a few weeks later that the President had invited the NAM to join the AFL-CIO in preparing for a summit meeting was a sure sign that nothing would come of the venture. Actually nothing did come of it. The summit idea didn't come to life until a new administration took over in Washington. Then President Kennedy bypassed the NAM and set up a very competent tripartite committee in the Executive Department. A precious year's time had been wasted.

Personally, I am inclined to think that collective bargaining as established in this country was never meant to cope with problems of inflation, balance of international payments and the consequences of automation. I have a feeling that our labor-management relations have been based on the competitive concept of a capitalistic system; that it was widely believed that in their negotiations labor and management could not possibly do anything but serve the general welfare, since the forces of competition would keep both parties on the reservation. I am afraid that this assumption is no longer verified, especially today under the strains of the cold war. I suspect that the assumption would sooner or later have been proved invalid even if the cold war had never erupted, because, over the years, American industry and American labor have become so organized and powerful that to some extent at least they can blunt the laws of competition and defy the law of supply and demand.

Such power is not a bad thing, since, as both Pope Leo XIII and Pope Pius XI taught, competition, though useful within limits, cannot be allowed to become the sole regulating force in the economy. The problem is to use this power constructively. Can labor and management so employ it within the traditional limits of collective bargaining that they will promote the general welfare as well as their own interests, or is some new institution needed that will enable unions and employers to function with greater consciousness of the common good? As things stand now, we are trying to supply for the deficiencies of collective bargaining by the device of a Labor-Management

25

Advisory Committee in the White House. President Kennedy is obviously hopeful that this committee will recommend constructive policies on automation, on wages and prices, and on a number of other matters that labor and management can follow. However, even if by some miracle this committee is able to agree on recommendations in these difficult fields, all the president can do is to appeal to labor and management to carry them out. He cannot compel compliance.

If the Cold War continues to grow in intensity, the experiment of the labor-management advisory committee, which is a promising one, will very likely prove to be inadequate. It may become necessary to impose wage and price controls. In that event, some of our leading industrialists may profitably ponder what might have happened if, two years ago, they had not rebuffed the AFL-CIO offer to go to the summit. In times of strain and crisis, the only alternative to government compulsion is labor-management cooperation. The NAM apparently forgot this.

CHAPTER 3

AUTOMATION AND MANPOWER IN THE 1960s

by SEYMOUR L. WOLFBEIN, *Deputy Assistant Secretary and Director of Automation and Manpower, U. S. Department of Labor*

ANY DISCUSSION OF the problem of automation and technological change in terms of human values must obviously start with the people themselves and how they now deploy themselves as members of the American work force and what the expectations are for the immediate years ahead.

To begin with, let's say that in terms of sheer numbers there is every indication that we will continue to get, as we have in the past, a substantial and significant increase in the population of the United States. We began this decade with about 180,000,000 people; we can expect to end the 1960s with close to 210,000,000, an increase of about 15 per cent.

Now it is important for us to understand that we will be getting different kinds of growth among different parts of our population. Certainly one of the outstanding sectors of the population in this respect is represented by the youth. Some idea of the importance of this sector of our population can be shown as follows: Between 1946—the first full peacetime year after World War II—and the beginning of 1960, 55,000,000 children were born in this country. As we have already indicated, when the census was taken in 1960, we were found to have 180,000,000 people. Note, therefore, this very important fact: just about one out of every three persons alive and kicking in the United States today wasn't even around at the end of World War II. All of us who are reflecting upon or are practitioners in the general field which we are discussing tonight must, therefore, take into account this overriding fact. Coming up to meet us during this decade is a surpassingly large sector of people with new goals, new hopes, new aspirations.

Look, for example, at the trend among those young people becoming eighteen years of age. This, of course, is a critical age group. It is the average age at which the American male makes his first full-time entry into the labor market. Back in 1950 we had about two million people becoming eighteen years of age each year. Now the figure is close to three million and by 1965 it will reach almost four million a year.

Incidentally, for those in the population who have children who will want to go into college in 1965, our advice is simple and unequivocal: buy a college.

Now every population increase brings with it, of course, a corresponding increase in the number of people in the labor force. We expect, during the decade of the 1960s, to get a net increase of about 13,500,000 in the American labor force—that is, from about 73,500,000 to about 87,000,000. This will be the largest 10-year jump for American workers in our history. But big as this increase is, the significant story is in the differential contributions made by the different age groups to the uptrend in the labor force for the next ten years. If one makes the 13,-500,000 net increase equal to 100 per cent, this is the way the labor force increase of the 1960s will distribute itself:

Total labor force 100%
Age 14-24 46
Age 25-34 13
Age 35-44 1
Age 45 and over 41

The manpower posture of any country changes from time to time and the decade that we are now embarking upon is going to be quite different from what it was in the 1950s. We will be getting a huge increase in the number of very young workers, a substantial increase in the so-called older workers, and a very small increase among workers in the central age groups. As a matter of fact, in one of them—age group 35-44—there will actually be a diminution of numbers between the beginning and the end of the current decade.

These figures, needless to say, present both a challenge and a promise. It means that we have to absorb into employment an enormous number of new young workers; in fact, the gross number of new job entrants during the 1960s will total the unprecedented and unparalleled figure of 26,000,000. Each of these 26,000,000 will be a young aspirant for a job consonant with his or her talents, aptitudes, interests, and motivations. Will we find the job opportunities for them—especially under the impact of automation and technological change? This certainly represents one of the major human challenges in the immediate years ahead for us.

At the same time, however, note the fact that we will actually have a deficit in an age group from which we usually draw our executive, managerial, supervisory personnel—an age group which already has a considerable amount of career development. This is why so many of us think that with good manpower management and utiliza-

29

tion and training we do have a good chance for absorbing the new young workers coming up this decade.

Finally, no discussion of the manpower situation, past, present, or future, can be made without reference to another group, called women. The pattern developing in postwar America has been as follows: Young ladies get their education and training, enter the labor force in rather significant proportions, exit upon marriage and childbearing, but then reenter in considerable numbers and percentages when the children are well along in their schooling. Already 1 out of every 2 women age 45-54 is in the labor force. Our expectations are that by 1970 we will have about 30 million women in the labor force, 25 per cent more than in 1960, and they will account for 1 out of every 3 workers in the United States. These, then, are the dimensions of our upcoming manpower supply: a very large number of the young, a very large number of the old, a relatively smaller number in the central age groups, and many more women.

Let's turn briefly now to what we think is going to be the demand side of the picture during the current decade. The important point to be made here can be put very briefly and simply. Since 1950 we have been the only country in the world which actually has more of its workers employed in the production of services than in the production of all the tangible goods that we need. In other words, if you put on one side all the American workers engaged in agriculture, in mining, in manufacturing, and in construction, we find that they total fewer than those workers engaged in trade, service, finance, insurance, transporation, and government. And sure enough, in 1957 we found that for the first time we were the only country in the world which actually has more white-collar workers than blue-collar workers; that is, we have more people employed as professional, managerial, clerical and sales personnel than all the skilled, semi-skilled, and unskilled workers put together. Now this is of enormous importance to the topic we are discussing to-night. The reason why we have a majority of our workers in the service-producing, white-collar sectors of the American economy is, in my opinion, that we can afford to have that kind of industrial and occupational distribution. We can afford to have this deployment of our labor force because of the extraordinary increases which have taken place in our productivity. It is in the goods-producing sectors that tremendous increases in output per man hour have occurred in the last generation, and we simply need fewer people to put out the enormous complex of goods that we have available to us.

To put it another way. In this country in the last half century, we have tripled the gross national product per capita. This is another way of saying that in the last fifty years we have increased threefold the amount of goods and services available to every man, woman, and child.

Now if you will reflect, you will see that there are only three ways in which a country can score up a remarkable record such as this. The first is to have an increase in the proportion of the population in the labor force. But this did not happen. Interestingly enough, the proportion of the population which works today in the United States is approximately the same as it was fifty years ago, although, of course, major changes have taken place within different groups of the population, e.g., a decline among the young, an increase among the women, etc.

The second way is to increase the number of hours that workers put in; yet, as we all know, just the opposite occurred in this country in the past half century. In other words, we have tripled the gross national product per capita with the same proportion of the population in the labor force working many fewer hours.

We come, therefore, to the third way—the way, of course, in which we made this achievement—through an increase in the output per man hour. So as we look ahead in the 1960s, it comes as no surprise to find that our research projects show a greater relative increase in the service-producing sectors of the American economy, especially, again, under the impact of automation and technological development.

What will these continuing trends mean to us? As one tries to find some continuity, some meaningful thread which can tie this package together, one comes, I think, inalterably to the matter of education and training. I think it is possible to say, with as much certainty as one can, that one of the areas of job opportunities which will continue to go down considerably is that represented by unskilled jobs. Automation and technological change keep cutting down the number of these jobs. In fact, the unskilled occupations represent the only job figure, outside of farming, of course, which has actually experienced not only a relative decline over the years but an absolute decline as well, and there is nothing in the offing which is going to change this trend.

This represents a very important lesson which must be imparted as effectively as possible into the counseling and guidance process. In our schools we must get the message across that higher education and training attainment is necessary, not only in terms of economic values, in its importance to citizenship, but also in terms of the hard facts of the American job market. And in this connection, I think that one of the most serious challenges facing us over the next years is represented by the fact that out of the 26,000,000 new young workers expected to come upon the job market in that period, fully 7,500,000 will be dropouts—that is, they will not have had a high school education. For them the prognosis is negative, indeed. Since their job outlet is perforce the unskilled trades, it is not surprising to find that they have the highest unemployment rates—rates which are currently running at 30 per cent.

What we see on the horizon in terms of automation, productivity, and new technology makes their job future all the darker and one of the steps that we think has to be taken immediately at the state and local and community levels is to increase the holding power of the schools. In this connection, let me note that all of the studies made in this field indicate that the young person drops out of school mostly because he does not find meaningful courses of instruction. Some, of course, fall out because of financial reasons; some, of course, fall out because they do not have the ability; but the overwhelming majority drop out —according to themselves, according to their teachers, according to their parents—because of a lack of meaningful courses of instruction. This is particularly true, of course, in the general field of vocational instruction. And this is particularly distressing because all of our figures indicate that we will need more and more skilled craftsmen. In fact, our projections call for an increase in the need for 5,000,000 more skilled craftsmen during the decade of the 1960s, and we are not now getting the required number.

The dimension of education and training is also very clear when one looks at the structure of unemployment today. As you all know, for the past year we have been announcing record levels of employment on the one hand and record levels of unemployment on the other. For example, between the spring of 1960 and the spring of 1961, there was a decline of 1,000,000 in the number of factory workers. Yet during that very same period of time, total employment rose by 800,000; this, mark you, in the face of a 1,000,000 drop in factory payrolls. The reason, of course, was a corresponding increase in the number of people employed in such service-producing activities as trade, service, finance, and state and local government, especially in the field of teaching.

It comes as no surprise, therefore, to find that there are certain sectors of our population which stand out very clearly as making up what we call the structurally unemployed. The attached table shows the composition of the more than 1,000,000 workers who had a record of continuous joblessness of six months or more in July, 1961. Note the disproportinate share from the unskilled workers, from the semi-skilled workers, from the Negro, from the older worker, and from the very young who are mostly drop-outs. Here, too, I think one of the major problems is that of education and training. These are the groups which bear the brunt of structural changes generated in part by automation and technological development, and we think that education and training and retraining and skill development represent one of the major pathways toward the solution of this problem. It is by no means a panacea. It must be accompanied by higher levels of economic growth and employment. But higher levels of economic activity themselves will not eliminate these pockets of unemployment.

The matter of education and training also applies to one other important point, again made especially important because of automation. More and more of the labor force are called upon to make relatively quick changes in their skills. In fact, I would say that one major dimension of education is to prepare the individual to withstand the inevitable conflicts which will occur in the relationship between what he learns and what he will be called upon to do. It has become almost impossible really to prepare and train people for specific occupations which they can embark upon and work in for the rest of their lives. Change is the key word, and what we need is a flexible,

COMPOSITION OF PERSONS ACTIVELY SEEKING WORK
FOR 27 WEEKS OR MORE

July 1961

Total number: 1,026,000

Group	Per cent distribution	
	Unemployed 27 weeks or more	In civilian labor force
Total	*100.0%*	*100.0%*
White	75.5	88.8
Negro	24.5	11.2
Total	*100.0*	*100.0*
Under 25 years of age	21.2	20.9
25-44	36.3	41.5
45 and over	42.5	37.6
Total	*100.0*	*100.0*
Professional technical	1.3	10.0
Farmers	.3	3.8
Managers, officials	2.1	9.5
Clerical	10.5	14.3
Sales	3.7	6.4
Skilled craftsmen	12.9	12.9
Semiskilled operatives	29.8	18.0
Private household workers	2.6	3.1
Other service workers	11.6	9.7
Farm laborers	.9	4.7
Unskilled industrial workers	16.7	6.3
No previous work experience	7.6	1.3
Total	*100.0*	*100.0*
Agriculture	1.3	9.0
Wage and salary	1.0	3.2
Self-employed and unpaid family	.3	5.8
Nonagriculture	91.1	89.8
Wage and salary	89.1	80.1
Forestry, fishing, mining	1.5	.9
Construction	10.2	6.1
Manufacturing	38.4	24.8
Durable goods	26.6	13.4
Primary metals	6.8	1.6
Autos	4.2	1.2
Other metals	10.7	7.4
Other durables	4.9	3.2
Nondurable goods	11.8	11.4
Transportation	5.9	6.4
Trade	14.5	15.1
Finance, service	14.2	22.0
Public administration	4.3	4.7
Self-employed and unpaid family	2.0	9.7
No previous work experience	7.6	1.3

maneuverable, adaptable labor force, responsive to the changes which will inevitably come with the impact of automation and technological change.

Today's want ads call for experience in data telemetry, microminiaturization, transistorized circuitry—job titles all but unknown a half dozen years ago, and this is just a harbinger of things to come.

The dimension of education and training finally is also directly relevant to one other point we want to discuss this evening, namely, the ethical and moral implications of automation in a free and democratic society. I look upon education and training and retraining as giving people a turn at bat. To be more technical, what it does is to increase the degree of freedom of choice of individual actions and it seems to me that this is the essence of what we want to achieve in our society, namely, a maximization of the degree of freedom of choice which an individual has in relation to just about all aspects of his life: where he lives, how he spends his income, how he works. And what education and training and skill development do, in a very specific and concrete way, is exactly that. They add to the adaptability and the maneuverability and the flexibility to which we alluded, and this is important not only in terms of the job market, but in terms of the individual himself.

CHAPTER 4

ETHICS AND
ECONOMIC SECURITY

by REV. DENNIS J. COMEY, S.J., *Director of St. Joseph's College (Philadelphia) Institute of Industrial Relations*

MAY I CLAIM an academic privilege to use a few moments to highlight observations which may be dreadfully obvious? The basic premise is that the usefulness of prefatory notes lies in establishing the same basic meaning for terms current in any discussion of collective bargaining.

We may start with agreement that a sheer analysis of human nature inevitably leads to the conclusion that man has an obligation to be social, to formulate his ideas and ideals in terms of others, to adjust his plans with due regard to their impact on the rights of others. A next step is easy. Because rights grow out of obligations, the postulate is sound that man has a right to be social. To give this premise a more specific meaning, we can agree that man has a right to join with others in the prosecution of a worthwhile goal in order that together men may achieve a benefit or benefits which must elude individual grasp.

This right is known as the right of association. Among workers it is called the right to organize. Usage has effected that the right to organize is hailed as a peculiar and exclusive prerogative of those who work for wages. Not so. With equal warrant the right may be properly

37

claimed by a Boy Scout troop, a ladies' sewing circle or a professional football team. The right to organize is exercised by the National Association of Manufacturers and by the Boilermakers' Union.

For our purposes it should help to accept the right to organize as a natural right. It is rather important to recognize that the right of association or the right to organize is the basis of collective bargaining.

However, a caution may be suggested. Allowing that the term may be loosely used, an exacting analyst might not concede that the right to bargain collectively is so well supported as the right to organize. A halting reflection reminds us that, in a sterner sense, rights are personal. Even so, such hair-splitting does not imply any challenge to the need for or the value of collective bargaining. Characterize the bargaining process as an effective means of implementing the right to organize. When company and union are organized, their representatives join forces in a shared effort to devise a joint solution of common problems. The descriptive definition will suit our present need.

Admittedly this approach to an earthy problem is theoretical and idealistic. No apology is indicated. There is no need to be misled by the more popular cult which pedestals the practical man. There is nothing truly practical unless it is based on a sound theory. And, conversely, if a theory is sound, it must be practical.

The pseudo-practical men of our day have debauched collective bargaining into a nasty economic grab for spoils; they have made the bargaining process an exercise of a magician's art, a contest in trickery and deception. A social-minded motive is scorned, reputed a luxury. Because so heavy an emphasis has been given to the economic detail, greed has been given its head. True enough, pennies and their fractions may become important and disputed issues. Earnest negotiators will not exclude the economic factor, but will not make it exclusive. For bargaining's true goal is human happiness, pride of accomplishment, comfort and convenience in the home, the education of children. These and related aims are capsuled under freedom and security. All these are to be measured by ethical standards. The economic detail is not robbed of its importance because it is a means rather than an end in itself.

The pessimist moans that collective bargaining has failed. Chesterton's observation that Christianity has not failed because it has not been tried, is applicable to bargaining. Hagglers have been allowed to establish a pattern that reflects neither bargaining nor a truly collective effort.

Yet a sound bargaining spirit has been instrumental in bringing about a major social revolution. Economic improvement has been authored by social-minded men, guided by sound moral principles.

To put into perspective the first stage of this revolution, we must reach back to the end of the last century. In 1891, when Leo XIII gave the encyclical *Rerum Novarum* to the world, his key teaching was embodied in an urgent plea that the workingman be paid a proper wage. In the immediately ensuing years, thoughtful analysts found warrant to insist that the wage contract be just; that represented a minimum. Equity and decency were added. Then, too, stress was given to the worker's role as husband and father. The pope's appeal did not stem from mere economics; it gathered its force from human and humane considerations, from the findings of the ethical philosopher.

Even though worldly men were not too impressed by the emphasis given to a supernatural motive, a change of attitude slowly penetrated hiring and wage practices. As late as 1910, grumbling employers pompously announced that a dollar a day was enough for any working man. As a vacationing schoolboy in 1911, I worked in a braid factory, turning a seven-foot wheel from seven in the morning until nine at night. The weekly pay was $5.50. During the following summer I kept account of stock, worked fifty-five hours each week and was paid the munificent sum of fifteen cents per hour. The shocking fact was that this was considered a man's wage.

The change is startling. That type of wage practice is simply impossible today. It is so outdated that baby-sitters find it incredible. The full complement of causes may be elusive. But count it certain that we as a people became more consciously aware of rights and obligations stemming from elemental justice, and a major impetus came from *Rerum Novarum*. From 1891 to World War I, the teaching of Leo XIII filtered down through the Church, pulpit, and classroom podium. Reflective and social-minded analysts argued the case in periodicals and reviews. Through the many avenues of communication, the plea was made that the worker not be belittled as another commodity in a glutted market, that justice prescribed a becoming wage in order that a man be equipped to provide ordinary frugal comfort for his wife and children.

Currently we are paying a decent wage. Let it be allowed that in some industries and trades the wage rate falls well below the average. Even so, an overall estimate warrants the claim that today's wage-earner fares better than his father and grandfather, much better than hardworking men of other lands.

Scout any notion that this stage of social revolution should be credited to economists and their man-made rules. Not so. Penny-grudgers were routed because those who manage and those who labor were persuaded that wages must be tailored to an elemental justice. A happy discovery was that good ethics proved to be good economics.

The second stage of our social revolution is more recent. About twelve or fourteen years ago a strike in steel dominated our news headlines.

As bargaining time approached its calendar date, the statistical experts in the industry prepared graphs and charts, aligned facts and figures in formidable array; they planned to prove and to prove conclusively that there was no warrant for an increase in wages.

However, in presenting contract proposals, the steelworker gave prior emphasis to a pension provision. Cries of horror rent the air. It was argued that an industry-provided pension must represent too heavy an impost, that it was reflective of a cradle-to-grave welfare program. Economically-minded critics branded the proposal as conducive to ruin.

The steelworker sought an economic benefit. But his argument was derived from an ethical claim. The union negotiators equivalently quoted the worker: "After I give you the best years of my productive power and reach a stage where I am physically incapable of continued work, you owe it to me to guarantee that I do not become a public charge." There was evoked the spectre of the poorhouse; there was pictured the aged and infirm worker almost literally begging for his bread.

To the everlasting credit of the industry executives let it be said they did not challenge the validity of this contention. They agreed that wages should allow a man and his family to live in reasonable comfort. A hardheaded appraisal dictated that existing wage rates thriftily used offered scant protection against the hazards of a wageless old age.

The strike that ensued spurted from disagreement concerning the economics of the pension. The focus of difference centered on the issue of the worker's contribution to the projected pension fund. Eventually bargainers gave

41

preference to human considerations, to the ethical warrant for a pension agreement. The economic problem was made secondary and was tailored to the more ethical measurement.

The effect in human terms is astounding. By habit we boast about the high standard of living which generally prevails in our United States. We forget that this lofty standard is not directly traceable to the wage paid the man who is husband and father. Commonly, young men and young women, impelled by their love of parents, contribute generously of their earnings to the maintenance and support of a cherished home. While the motive may be applauded, the practice had a damaging effect in that young people postponed marriage. Delay was accepted as the burden of caring for old folks.

Pension agreements have helped to eliminate this need. By reason of some continuing income, the ordinary requirements of old age are fulfilled. Our young people are marrying earlier, setting up their own homes, raising families. This development spells a tremendous benefit for both old and young; its advantage is not only ethical and moral, but its repercussions reach into the economic area.

Again, the personal freedom made possible by pensions is an impressive gain. If there is any quality of character thoroughly masculine, it is a sturdy sense of independence. Even the hasty stubbornness of a baby boy may more certainly represent the first surge of an independent spirit, a sense of self-reliance, the resourcefulness that betokens readiness to carry responsibility. The craving for independence does not fade in old age; in fact, passing years add spark to the quest.

Retirement for a hard-working man may provide the comfort that his sons and daughters will match the sacrifices made for them. But it pains him deep down inside that he cannot fend for himself. Lifetime habits are hard to change. It hurts that he must depend on his loved ones for the trifles that can make old age and idleness more tolerable.

The pension plan written into so many labor agreements does not finance luxurious living. But the retiree is privileged to exercise a comforting measure of independence. At least, he can equip himself with a cigar and a morning paper; he need not extend a beggar's hand for the price of a haircut.

True, the financial burden of establishing a pension fund may tax the employer's economic ingenuity. The investment pays rich dividends in the happiness shared by aging parents and their grown sons and daughters.

The third stage of our social revolution still occasions outbursts of grumbling complaint. Its evidence is the so-called welfare clause written into many labor agreements, the insurance written to protect a worker and his family against the incidence of sickness or surgery, hospitalization or balancing income. There is no valued contribution to our knowledge in the growl that all such fringe benefits cost money; that counter is trite. The more important concern should be the benefit bought.

In bargaining for a welfare clause, the worker argues: "I have a right, given me by Almighty God, and an obligation imposed on me by God to provide ordinary medical care for myself, my wife, and my children." Since that premise is unassailable, the petitioner continues: "If I can't exercise my right and fulfill my obligation by means of my wage, there must be another source available to me." Anticipating rebuff, the pleader insists that economic obstacles must be upended; he refuses to agree that the providence of God is subject to dubious laws of economics.

Again, resolution of difficulties was effected by the bargaining of men equipped with the vision and insight to appreciate the broader, social issue. The welfare agreement acknowledges that the man is the head of the family, that the family is the unit of society, that even the economic prosperity of society hinges on the stability of the family. The cost is trifling when posed against the benefit gained.

A fourth stage of our social revolution is exemplified by the guaranteed annual wage sought a few years ago by the United Auto Workers. As was to be expected, the habitual viewers-with-alarm jutted hands upward in horror as they grumbled: "Now we'll pay men for not working." The picture was drawn of a laid-off machinist headed for Florida and leisured, deep-sea fishing, all financed by a workless wage. The oversimplification confused the issue. Certainly the petitioning worker entertained a much weightier concern.

The problem confronting the wage-earner was challenging, yet it defied all his ingenuity. He expressed himself forcibly: "I have sunk my roots in this community. Here I have my home and its mortgage, my church, a school for my children. I have a boy in college and I want to keep him there in order that he may not have to work so hard as his father. I want to provide milk and shoes for my little nine-year-old girl. What happens if I am laid off for some reason utterly beyond my control? Do I lose my home? Is my boy's education to be foreshortened? Who will tell a little girl that she may not have a new dress for her birthday?"

The Auto Workers detailed the challenge in bargaining with the Ford Motor Company. It may have surprised the union's negotiators that Henry Ford II had anticipated the plea, had weighed and weighted the persuading argument, had made solution the goal of a three-year study project. The human factor sparked an answer. In spite of economic roadblocks, Ford devised what we now call Supplemental Unemployment Benefits.

The benefit is incalculable. In terms of monied protection, a laid-off worker may draw approximately sixty-five per cent of his normal pay for a twenty-six-week period. The fears of pencilling pessimists give way to the certainty that hardships have been minimized. The supplemental pay allows no luxury; it cannot warrant extended Florida fishing. But the worker is enabled to keep up mortgage payments on his home, to keep his son in college, to sponsor the thrill of a new dress for a little girl. The SUB agreement may well be classified as advanced social thinking.

Surely the lesson to be learned from experience dictates that the emphatically human problem lurking in all labor-management relations is not to be resolved solely by economic adjustments. These are important, of course. But the bookkeeper, the accountant, the economist must not become so obsessed with addition and subtraction that people are forgotten or ignored. Let the pencil wielder move over to make room for the ethical philosopher. Let management and labor vie with each other in promoting happiness.

Interestingly enough, the great advances made through the past half century were promoted by human and humane considerations. Wages, pensions, welfare programs, unemployment allowances reflect a deeper social consciousness. True, the employer mumbles and grumbles about spiralling costs, but he knows a deep satisfaction of soul for having supported the impelling ambitions of his employees.

Whether aware of it or not, management and labor bargainers achieved their most noteworthy success when they assumed the philosopher's role. Ethical norms have prevailed over economic rigidities.

At each stage of our social revolution, the professional economists predicted appalling ruin. They objected to the

45

ten-hour day and the eight-hour day; they foresaw only disaster in wage increases; welfare, insurance, hospitalization programs were branded as an invitation to national bankruptcy; unemployment protections clashed with cherished theory.

The economic Jeremiah has proved himself one hundred per cent wrong. We are today the most prosperous nation on the face of the earth. Working men and their families live better than ever in our history. Children are bigger and stronger because they are well fed, well equipped for the uncertainties of the future, because they are better schooled. Meantime, company and corporation profits continue to explode into higher levels. Why the pained moans of unhappy analysts and critics?

All this is evidence of a nightmarish inflation? Maybe. Maybe not. The wizardry of experts is dead-ended by the need of sharp definition. Inflation is no longer a shortage of commodities coupled with an abundance of money. Explanations of what is currently called inflation vary according to the convictions or prejudices of the complainer. A sense of balance is needed: money is not so sacred that its values must forever go unchanged; people are truly sacred, and money is a tool. Why not exult that employers, employees and their dependents are today enjoying convenience and comfort unknown to an older generation?

Incessantly, the ghost of socialism is invoked—without warrant. It is surely integral to any true form of socialism that there be public, and reductively governmental, control or domination or dictation. A most intriguing feature of our social advance is that government played a decidedly minor role. Progress must be attributed to thoughtful and reflective men who gathered about a bargaining table, raised wages, established pension funds, wrote insurance to provide medical care, devised unemployment safeguards. Government followed the lead of enterprising negotiators.

Against the danger that glory-seekers may distort history, it is emphatic that the great achievements of the past fifty years must not be claimed by any one group. Labor's insistence on a crusader's victory is misplaced. Damage is done to the future by the more oratorical claim that benefits had to be wrung in droplets from grudging employers. Unfair. Bow in respect to far-sighted businessmen motivated by an honest concern for workers and their families. Save a niche, too, for teachers and authors who crystallized ideas and ideals, who helped to translate dreams into real accomplishments.

This peek into the recent past warrants a glimpse of the future. The wonders of automation may be frightening; its immediate impact on workers and jobs is not softened by the assurance that long-range benefits promise a burgeoning prosperity for all. Earnest diagnosis of problems, a continuing search for remedy, honest evaluation of economic and engineering developments must be undertaken. The hope for people is that bargainers have learned that truth and honesty, justice and fair play are as important as ledger columns and automation's feedback. The prospect is encouraging. For success through a half century must embolden men of vision.

CHAPTER 5

LABOR
AND AUTOMATION

by ABRAHAM WEISS, *Director of Research*
International Brotherhood of Teamsters

I AM PLEASED that a great Catholic institution devoted to preparing young men for priesthood is interested in automation and its problems. I share the view, which I believe you hold, that religious bodies have a real stake in morality, social and economic areas of life; that religious bodies are not satisfied with generalizations, such as love thy neighbor as thyself.

The discussions about automation touch at the root of all considerations for an equitable and moral social and economic order. Problems of full employment, better wages, fair working conditions and a high living standard are fundamental to the maintenance of world peace and to the preservation of democracy in America.

Religious bodies are in accord in their concern with the ethical undergirding of our social framework. They maintain that a healthy economy is indispensable to a wholesome society. To quote a phrase, "where there is no bread, there is no law." Religious groups are conscious of the many inadequacies, injustices and inequalities which still prevail in our social and economic structure and in the many points of friction between labor and management, the two great pillars of our industrial system.

49

We in the trade unions are hopeful that there will be increasing understanding and respect between labor and management on the issue of automation. We look forward to greater assumption of responsibility by government and the public for securing and improving the common life of our society.

Economic Background

Automation is feared today because it is rolling into high gear at a time when our economy is generating new jobs at a slower rate than the growth of our labor force. At a time when we have gone through four recessions in the last decade, when unemployment is at higher levels after each recession, when joblessness rises from month to month, when private industry now produces fewer man-hours of work than in 1953, when manufacturing output has risen 17 per cent since 1953 but employment has dropped 5 per cent, workers properly feel concern over job security and employment opportunities.

The U. S. Department of Labor expects the labor force to increase by 13,500,000 between 1960 and 1970, as compared to 8,900,000 in the previous decade. Secretary of Labor Arthur Goldberg has stated that the economy must provide 10,500,000 new jobs next year. At the present time, there are no signs that these jobs will be available—next year, or during the next decade. Certainly the economic climate seems to hold out little hope for work opportunities. Without a much greater increase in jobs than has been taking place in recent years, our unemployment problem obviously will become a serious threat to our whole future.

These economic facts of life serve as a background for understanding workers' reactions to automation, which in turn motivate their unions' attitudes and policies. You all realize, I know, that psychological factors have significant economic effects. Whether we are management or union officials, we cannot afford to discount human reaction to change.

Over 85 per cent of our income earners are on a wage or salary basis. Today, the worker's only means of providing sustenance for himself and his family is to find employment and try to retain it. Is it a wonder, then, with the uncertainties produced by rapid technological change and the ever-present threat of recurrent recessions with their mass unemployment, that the worker attempts to avoid the consequences of joblessness?

Automation represents progress. Agreed! Therefore, the argument runs, it is unethical and antisocial to oppose it. But look at the individual worker. He has acquired skills and a family and he is over forty, yet he is called on to sacrifice himself for society. Where are the ethics in this situation? It is thus a question of individual rights and protection against industry's profit rights and an unsympathetic society. There *are* individual costs involved. It is *not* a simple question.

Workers react to mechanization or automation in the following ways:

(1) *Fear of Unemployment*—Some employees are going to be displaced from their present jobs.

(2) *Increased Feeling of Insecurity*—The very fact of change is upsetting and creates doubts over their future job security. They are suspicious in advance of changed work conditions, especially when they haven't participated in the decisions, and don't understand the reasons for the changes. Their suspicions are as strong whether the change affects them adversely or not, and justifiably so.

(3) *Resistance, Sometimes to the Point of Violence*—These fears create an attitude of resistance. Most

workers recognize the general principle that increased efficiency and productivity are the basis for an ever-improving standard of living for the employee as a worker and as a consumer. This they accept as long as they are not faced with the loss of their jobs. But when this threat becomes personal, their reaction is characteristically one of self-protection—in a variety of forms.

(4) *Workers Want an Opportunity to Run the New Machines and Equipment*—This feeling is, I think, self-evident.

These fears and feelings by workers create problems for union leaders as well as for management. Even though the union has established a general policy of not resisting but of accepting new methods of work, there is often strong opposition from workers who are affected or fear they will be affected by the change. This shows up in a variety of ways (stubborn grievances, slowdowns, etc.), and in workers' insistence on protective clauses the next time the contract is open. This forces unions into the position of trying to restrict and prevent management from introducing new methods to increase efficiency. Out of these conflicts of immediate interests come some of the most perplexing human relations problems for both management and the union.

These problems are further complicated by the failure of many managements to give as much time and study to the question of *how* changes are to be made, as they give to the question of *what* changes are to be made.

The Role of the Union

We recognize that progress, productivity and efficiency are vital to the welfare of our members and the industries which employ them. But as trade unionists and as Americans, we consider human beings and their welfare more important than efficiency. The well-being of our people is an integral part of our economic progress and national security. Equally important, we must recognize that people without jobs cannot provide a market for the products or services of automated industry.

We know that there is no self-adjusting labor market mechanism which acts automatically to provide jobs. We believe that it is unjust and antisocial to make workers shoulder the entire burden of "efficiency" or technological change. Rapid and uncontrolled technological change can disrupt the lives of workers and their families and our nation. We must urge that thought be given to programs for reducing the harmful effects of such dynamic growth. We cannot afford to repeat previous mistakes of our industrial history. No technological change which is made at the expense of workers is true technological progress. We cannot afford to sell our human values simply to get more efficiency. The costs of assisting human beings (and communities) to adjust to changing technology should be included as an important part of the total investment costs in the new technology.

It is appropriate to quote from *Mater et Magistra*, Pope John XXIII's Social Encyclical: "Social progress should accompany and be adjusted to economic development so that all classes of citizens can participate in the increased productivity." This applies to workers retained on the job and to workers displaced.

In essence, what we are asking for is a high degree of social and economic responsibility by industry and by the society as a whole, in effect, a weighing of the human costs of displacement.

Social and economic progress are not automatic. The union must insure that its members are not hurt. This is our role, and we cannot and will not shirk it.

It is this apparent conflict between economic efficiency

*and social justice which our society must solve if we are to
avoid economic and social catastrophe.*

We view automation as a great promise, provided there
is a strong labor movement to see to it that automation's
promise of widespread abundance is made a reality for the
benefit of people. Machines can do everything except buy
what they make; it takes sufficient money in peoples' pockets all the year round to keep cash registers ringing.

In theory, technological unemployment is supposed to
be merely transitional; the man so unemployed should
soon be reabsorbed. But the promise of the theory is of
little solace to the hungry worker when he sees the employment offices crowded with job seekers who cannot find
work. And what about the displaced worker whose skill
has been automated along with his job? And the theory
does not explain industry's opposition to hiring older
workers who have been technologically unemployed. What
happens to seniority rights, equities built up in retirement plans, savings plans, and other benefits on the old
job?

We do not resist automation, but we want to cushion
its effect on labor. From labor's point of view, we want to
reconcile, as far as possible, the continual growth of automatic technology with job security. We wish to alleviate
the hardships of those displaced by automation and to
protect the employment opportunities, earnings, and work
conditions of those retained on the job. Automation
makes possible increased productivity. The fruits of such
productivity should be shared with workers. Only through
increased purchasing power can the increased ability to
produce be matched by a corresponding ability to consume what is produced.

A free democratic private enterprise system must never
lose sight of the central purpose of its economy: satisfying
human needs. Production is *not* the ultimate goal; profits

54

per se are *not* the measure of economic health. We measure progress in terms of how people live, of their economic security, of their ability to provide education for their children, of the degree to which production of goods contributes to a happier life and a more wholesome community.

We in the trade unions recognize that automation may produce long-range gains. Improved living standards have been made possible by increased knowledge and increased productivity. At the same time, we must call attention to the fact that this is a *long-range* process, and that the *immediate* impact of automation does raise certain *immediate* social and economic problems for workers.

It is here that collective bargaining—the unions' tool— enters. A variety of collective bargaining contract provisions have been developed:

(1) *Higher Wages*—to assure workers a direct, sure, and speedy share in the benefits of technological advance and so that consumers can buy the products of industry.

   Unions may have to consider contract clauses which provide for sharing in savings of lower labor unit costs; or mechanization increases (aside from general wage increases) which represent an equitable portion of the wage cost of labor displaced by automation.

(2) *Shorter Hours*—with no loss in take-home pay, to create more jobs. This may be through shorter workday or workweek, longer vacations, more holidays.

(3) *Annual Wage*—to maintain purchasing power; to force industry to plan more rigorously, so as to minimize displacement.

   Technology requires our system to become primarily a consumption economy. The guaranteed annual

55

wage provides an effective market for the goods and services of automated industry.

The West Coast Longshoremen's Agreement, for example, guarantees that no layoffs will result from mechanization and workers are assured a minimum wage based on a thirty-five-hour week.

The International Brotherhood of Electrical Workers has negotiated a flat, unequivocal job and wage rate guarantee for workers with five years or more of service. (Normal turnover, retraining and transfers are used to take care of reduced manpower needs.)

(4) *Dismissal Pay*—as partial recompense for loss of job and equity rights built up by length of service and to tide the worker over the immediate job-loss period.

Similar in intent are supplementary unemployment benefits (SUB), which guarantee laid-off workers about 65 per cent of their past take-home earnings for periods of from twenty-six to fifty-two weeks.

(5) *Seniority*—By enlarging the area for protecting seniority rights, we seek to protect the worker from changes in job classification—since automation changes the number of employees needed to perform a particular function may require new skills, may combine several departments through different work flows. Interplant transfer rights to other company plants and preferential rehiring are additional seniority safeguards.

(6) Retraining of displaced workers by the company, at company expense to permit workers to accommodate to the new technology, as in the following contract provision for office workers:

When the installation of mechanical or electronic office equipment . . . will have an effect on the job status of employees, management will notify the . . . union . . . in advance of such installation. In the event such . . . equipment is installed, management shall provide reasonable training arrangements for the employees who were displaced from their positions by such installation in order that such employees may have an opportunity to become qualified as required for newly established jobs on such installations. The balance of the employees whose jobs are discontinued will be given reasonable training in order that they become qualified to take other jobs in the unit to which their seniority entitles them.

(7) *Pensions*—greater benefits; earlier retirement age; early vesting rights.

(8) *Advance Notice* to the union and adequate joint consultation so that changes can be worked out *before* workers are displaced.

These collective bargaining provisions, and others, constitute, in essence, a form of social cost of automation for industry. They call for a high degree of social responsibility by management. *A number of companies have recognized their responsibilities in this area—and I salute them for it.*

But these collective bargaining arrangements between a company or an industry and a union (or unions) are essentially only shock absorbers or stop-gaps. They constitute merely the first line of defense against automation unemployment. Essentially, they are designed to cope with the problem of "temporary" technological unemployment, rather than a situation where a man's job literally disappears under automation.

Unfortunately, collective bargaining contract protections cannot create essential job opportunities. Collective bargaining *alone* cannot cope with the tremendous pressures of automation-induced unemployment. The complexity of the problem calls for an effort beyond that of any single union, or single company, or single industry, or combined labor-management effort.

Labor and management should continue to seek solutions to the labor problems flowing out of automation. But these private solutions, in the final analysis, can only be limited and temporary.

National Economic Policies Must Support Collective Bargaining on Automation

After all, collective bargaining affects only a fraction of our total economy. Other factors, such as tax, monetary, credit, fiscal, and budget policy are more far-reaching in their consequences. We must, therefore, develop a proper national economic and social environment to make the achievements of collective bargaining and labor-management cooperation successful.

If technological progress is to be orderly, we must tackle the unemployment problem promptly on a *national* scale. The national well-being requires it; the continued existence of our present social and economic order demands it. Full employment must be our goal if we are to avoid the nightmare problem of displacement and chaos created by technological "progress."

This calls for effective implementation of the Employment Act of 1946 so as to provide a constantly expanding economy both to generate jobs and to sustain buying power. We need *both* increased consumer purchasing power to match our growing productive capacity, and increased business investment to further create employment and stimulate consumption.

We need allied programs consisting of wage supports, tax measures, training and retraining programs, relocation subsidies, and other social security guarantees to technologically displaced workers and their families. But above all, there must be a job at the end of the line for those willing and able to work. Otherwise, the best social insurance systems and retraining and placement resources are of little use. This is why the full employment goal must be the capstone of our national policies.

In spite of our vaunted American standard of living, there are still millions of American families living on substandard incomes. In spite of our vast wealth, the gap between need and fulfillment in the public sector is enormous: in education, health, slum clearance, public housing, metropolitan redevelopment, and preservation and development of natural resources. When we build school classrooms, hospitals, public housing, and all other things our people need, private industry will have more business and people will enjoy full employment.

As a nation, we must constantly adjust our thinking to meet an age of greater abundance. Automation will provide that greater abundance. Automation can be used to serve men and to free men. But if, because of automation, workers lose their jobs, *or are never hired,* then the central purpose of our economic activity in a democratic society is defeated. Economic progress must be equated with human needs. For this, we need a constantly expanding economy, to absorb both new workers and those displaced by technical advances. Full employment is the answer!

Unemployment Threatens Economic Chaos

Change the unemployment level a bit and the problem of technological displacement changes from a relatively manageable question of adjustment to a social catastrophe of alarming proportions, in which *orderly* technological progress becomes impossible.

Workers have a right to a fair share of the fruits of the

nation's expanding productivity, which automation will accelerate. Without a proper balance between production and consumption, full employment and prosperity are impossible and we reach an economic dead end.

Surplus wheat can be stored. Surplus workers—and that is what automation is creating—cannot! Our members are not accustomed to eating on a long-run basis. Their bills have to be paid today. They cannot obtain credit on the expectation of a job two years from now. All they know is that their jobs are evaporating and they are left high and dry.

People cannot buy unless they work. Industry cannot sell its products and services unless people have money. Industry looks to the consumer to keep the economy going. Eliminating productive jobs eliminates the consuming market for that and other products. One cannot produce wealth with machines alone.

If we can develop crash programs for missiles and exploration of outer space, we can and must plan to solve the problems flowing out of automation. We must devise and develop tools to wipe out the spectre of chronic mass unemployment—the sentence of economic death. Our nation faces no challenge so great—if we are to maintain the stability of our economy and way of life. If past policies and methods are inapplicable to today's technology, let us devise new ones. (In the meantime, the worker looks to his union for protection—and the union is not going to let him down!)

Why should we have full employment only in time of war? Full employment to fulfill life is ever so much more important than full employment to destroy life and property in war. Certainly in time of peace there is work to be done—job-providing work—to improve the well-being of people and the nation. Let us set our sights for abundance, not scarcity. Let us gear our policies for full production, not under-utilization of capacity and facilities. Let public investment join private enterprise in supplying people's needs! The essential public enterprise operations which will create new and badly needed jobs are: education, health, slum clearance, public housing, metropolitan re-development, and preservation and development of natural resources.

There is no private profit in the building of public schools, in the proper training and remuneration of teachers, in the building of hospitals, health research laboratories, and health training schools; in the demolition of the disease-ridden, crime-breeding slums, in the construction of dams to save water for irrigation and other uses, and for the generation of cheap electricity, with the by-products of reforestation, wildlife conservation, and recreation. These and similar projects not only fulfill the needs of the people, but they also create big new opportunities for private business and, therefore, for employment.

The basic answer to the problems created by automation lies in the prosperity of our country. If our economy is faltering, any solutions to the unemployment problem —whether automation-created or otherwise—are bound to be ineffective.

It is obvious that only increased "economic growth" can provide enough jobs for an increasing work force in our economy where, day by day, fewer workers are turning out more goods. As long as our economy expands, automation's impact on employment will be softened.

Recommendations

(1) Broaden the scope of the U. S. Employment Service to permit it to aid displaced workers in their transfer from area to area, with possible financial assistance in these transfers.

61

(2) Establish a joint commission composed of management, labor, and government to determine the actual impact of automation. No one really knows the depth and nature of the social implications of the automation programs now in operation, or forthcoming in the future. The commission should study the total impact of automation on our national, economic, political, and social structure, not with a view to stopping it, but with the view of meeting the needs of its progress.

(3) Government administration of a financial program aimed at retraining displaced employees. The program should be administered through the U.S.E.S.

(4) Lower the Social Security retirement age and pass "anti-moonlighting" legislation to prevent people holding two jobs. This would spread the work among more people. Higher pension benefits should be made available so that early retirement would not be so painful to the workers.

(5) Review and revise our tax and monetary policies to assure that they are stimulating economic growth and job-creating potential.

Such programs must be put into action as soon as possible. As I have already indicated, collective bargaining alone cannot shoulder the entire burden of coping with automation's problems.

Until we have such a national program, industries where technological changes are destined to be made may face strained labor relations. The result may well be collective bargaining settlements that produce restrictions on technological change.

Workers expect protection from their unions. And their unions—no matter how statesmanlike their leadership—

can have no choice but to seek to protect their members from being dumped onto our economic slag-heaps.

The central problem is unemployment, the threat of job displacement and job dislocation. Since the social and economic systems, as well as private enterprise, have abdicated any responsibilities for alleviating the economic and human problems directly associated with the individual worker and his employment security, he must, through his union, try to solve these problems for himself. Further, until more satisfactory methods are devised, workers will be insisting on protective clauses.

The drawbacks of technological progress must no longer be allowed to fall on the shoulders of single groups of workers. The human community is rich enough and the labor movement is strong enough to prevent this happening in the future. The *whole* of society enjoys the benefits of automation. The *whole* of society must, therefore, bear its costs.

We must put the working man or woman affected by the changing industrial process, rather than the process itself, at the center of our concern.

Unemployment is not an act of nature; it is an act of man. And it is by human action, sensible and compassionate, that we must cope with its hazards and develop the means not only of adequately compensating the displaced worker for the income he has lost but, more to the point, of furthering his reintegration, whenever possible, as a self-sustaining breadwinner in the economy.

CHAPTER 6

ETHICS, ECONOMICS, AND CHRONIC UNEMPLOYMENT IN THE MIDST OF AUTOMATED ABUNDANCE

by REV. WILLIAM J. BYRON, S.J.
Woodstock College

WHEN ETHICIANS AND economists meet to discuss the problem of unemployment here in the land of automated plenty, it is always useful to begin with a clear view of the human person around whom this discussion must necessarily turn. For depressed areas are inhabited by unemployed *people,* and in the face of continued automation, *people* will benefit or suffer (depending on the side of this debated issue you choose to defend). Consequently, both ethician and economist must know, first of all, who is unemployed and then agree to base their discussion of the problem on a mutually acceptable premise regarding the nature and dignity of the human person. How this dignity is to be recognized and served by public policy is an issue which divides the so-called liberal and conservative elements of our society. The Chamber of Commerce of the United States, famous for its conservative stance and opposition to most social legislation, had this to say by way of comment on "public aid":

In introducing proposed new minimum wage fixing legislation, Senator John Kennedy stated: "It has been said that the test of our belief in human dignity is the manner in which we treat those at the bottom of the economic ladder." Whoever said this we do not know; but it reflects a dubious attitude of paternalism, handouts and public succor. It is just possible, on the contrary, that in our public policies we will do more good by taking exactly the opposite attitude, admitting of course, the need of taking care of people in distress.[1]

It is important to realize, then, that despite agreement in the Judaeo-Christian tradition which recognizes the dignity of man as flowing from his origin, nature and destiny, there will be much latitude of view on how that dignity is to be acknowledged in practice.

In late 1959 and early 1960, a special Senate Committee on Unemployment Problems worked under the chairmanship of Senator Eugene J. McCarthy (D.—Minn.) and produced more than six thousand five hundred pages of hearings, readings, studies, and reports on the causes and conditions of unemployment in the United States. This committee was not empowered to report on pending legislation but simply to conduct a careful analysis of the problem of joblessness and present to the Senate a guide for action. The committee concluded that "class" rather than "mass" unemployment has characterized the past decade and it offered for remedial action general policy recommendations of a fairly conservative stripe.

> "Class" rather than "mass" unemployment has characterized the past decade. Unemployment is highest for young people, older workers, nonwhites, women, the unskilled, and the least educated. Improved vocational training and retraining programs are needed to help these groups.[2]

When the viewpoint shifts from the decade past to the

decade ahead, the prognosis for each of these troubled classes is somewhat grim.

"Younger workers" are those under twenty-five. Percentagewise, unemployment is higher here than in any other age group of the labor force. A disturbing shadow is cast over this already dark picture by the mounting numbers within this class. In the decade ahead, twenty-six million new young workers will enter the labor force, almost 40 per cent more than during the 1950s. "The vast increase in the number of new job seekers, unaccompanied by compensating withdrawals by other age groups, will put a severe strain upon the economy's capacity to absorb their energies and aspirations for productive lives." [3] Millions of these newcomers to the work force will be unskilled; many will be poorly and partially-educated dropouts from school. This multiplication of younger members of the work force gives us a first hint as to why the Labor Department regards manpower as the "Challenge of the Sixties." [4]

"Older workers" are people over forty-five. This group will grow by roughly 20 per cent in ten years, representing an increase of 5,500,000 over 1960. By 1970, more than 33,000,000 men and women over forty-five will belong to the labor force. Although older workers do not experience as high a rate of unemployment as do workers under twenty-five, when unemployment does hit a person past forty-five, he remains idle for longer periods of time and, in some cases, withdraws prematurely from the labor force. In other words, the older worker bears the major burden of chronic, long-term joblessness and remedies for chronic unemployment should be designed with the older worker in mind.[5] Can he be persuaded to sell his home (at a loss in areas of declining job opportunities), break social ties of long standing, retrain and relocate in an economy where jobs are scarce and applicants over forty-five are repeatedly bypassed at the hiring office? What can be done through union and management cooperation to finance retraining and relocation, to make seniority, health and pension benefits portable from job to job, region to region?

A larger proportion of women, particularly older women, will be working or seeking work in the decade ahead. The proportion of married women in the labor force is expected to rise sharply from the present level where already more than one-third of the married women between the ages of thirty-five and fifty-four are holding jobs outside the home. The continued introduction of automated bookkeeping, vending, clerical and other processes could produce a shortage of jobs for women. But even if the economy holds a job for every woman who wants one, there seems to be an ethical flaw in a system where the wife's income is a major contributor to the maintenance of the standard of living enjoyed by many American families. More immediate, personal considerations of an ethical nature might crop up in terms of neglected family responsibilities and unnecessary competition with those whose need for work is much greater. In the depressed areas, however, economic necessity fosters a high rate of female participation in the work force. The proportion of female employment in the Wilkes-Barre–Hazleton, Pa. area (a depressed anthracite coal region) is higher (45 per cent of total) than in practically any other labor market in the country. This means that the household roles are often reversed and the wife is the principal breadwinner. It is interesting to note how the mobility of capital is operative in this situation as needle and light assembly jobs seek out cheap female labor. This phenomenon both contributes to and is caused by the continued immobility of jobless men in these same areas.

When the work force is broken down into white and nonwhite components, the resultant unemployment figures reveal a sharp disadvantage for the Negro. The percentage of idle Negroes is usually more than double the corresponding rate for unemployed whites. Among men twenty-five to forty-four, the rate of unemployment was three times as high for Negro as for white workers in the spring of 1959. The adage that the Negro is the last to be hired and the first to be fired is verified by the characteristically longer stretches of involuntary Negro idleness. Negroes are caught by discrimination, lack of skills, immobility and insufficient education. Attempts to relieve the chronic distress of an area like Detroit cannot afford to ignore the racial composition of the labor market.

A geographic classification of this problem would situate most of the long-term unemployment in the upper-right quarter of the United States—roughly, east of the Mississippi River and north of the Tennessee-Kentucky line. In this quadrant, economic vitality is declining or just about holding its own while most of the economic growth in the United States is occurring in a sweeping crescent of states running roughly from Washington and Oregon, down through California, over across Nevada, Arizona, New Mexico, through Texas, Louisiana and into Florida. This is the life-line of prosperous "hard" spots in the future economy.[6]

Technologically displaced workers might be considered as a "class" of the unemployed. They populate most of the depressed areas in the Middle-Atlantic, East North-Central and Northeastern United States. They are also the people over whom the "work rules" and "job security" disputes arise during labor-management negotiations in industries where automation is increasing and unions are strong. The issue is one of "management's right to manage" over against the union's claim to a voice in the disposition of workers who are displaced by machines.

Finally, when the labor force is analyzed in terms of

skills, it is clear that the unskilled and uneducated feel the bite of automation and the burden of enforced idleness more than any other group. The unskilled and uneducated are overlooked by those who repeat the comforting ambiguity that "Automation will create more jobs than it destroys." High productivity in a growth economy can produce new jobs. Those who are displaced by automated productivity-increases will get these new jobs only if they are occupationally and geographically mobile. Mobility, especially geographic mobility, is least evident among the unskilled and uneducated. Unskilled workers change employers often enough, but they will have to acquire new and marketable skills if they are to keep ahead of automation.

There, in brief and broad outline, are the classes of people behind the unemployment statistics. With their interests, rights and dignity in mind, what can the planners do to attack the nation's unemployment problem? The McCarthy Committee Report sees a causal link between automation (defined as "mechanization of thought, sensory, and control processes"[7]) and persistent unemployment in the nation's depressed areas:

> Even if automation holds promise for the future, its short-term effects are obviously disturbing to individual displaced workers and nearly catastrophic to entire communities, such as those in the coal regions. And if a city the size of Detroit can be shaken by automation, no community in the country can be complacent about its effects.[8]

As has been indicated earlier in this chapter, an attempt will be made throughout the chapter to match up proposed remedies for unemployment with the people and communities which these remedies are intended to help. Special attention will be given to proposals for training, retraining and relocating the unemployed.

70

After examining classifications of the jobless, both economist and ethician will be well advised to review the difference between:

(1) Unemployment and displacement.

(2) Automation and mechanization.

(3) The impact of automation on the job and job holder.

We will take the third set first. Automation upgrades the job but not the man who holds the job. Walter Buckingham, director of the School of Industrial Management at the Georgia Institute of Technology, stressed this point in a paper prepared for the Joint Economic Committee of Congress.[9] He sees no evidence that automation upgrades workers generally in the sense of requiring a worker to be equipped with more intensive knowledge. More complicated machines do not necessarily require more complicated skills to tend them. "Although [many highly specialized workers] earn high wages because of their high productivity when working with machinery, their jobs could be performed by well-trained monkeys. A completely inexperienced worker can be trained in thirty minutes for more standard factory jobs." [10] This is a vital distinction which demands the attention of those who are planning retraining programs for the unemployed and vocational education for newcomers to the labor force. The displaced factory worker is hardly a likely candidate for retraining as a computer programer. As the analysis of our manpower experts indicates, professional, technical, and skilled workers will be in demand in the years ahead while unskilled labor will stand idle. Our planners, however, must understand that the degree of skill is measured by the length of time which it normally takes to learn the job, not by the expense or complexity of the machine being tended. When a machine operator becomes, after automation, a machine monitor, his job is upgraded but he and his skill are not. As a matter of fact, his economic security is now in greater jeopardy for the complex of machines which he now starts, watches and stops could easily be started, watched and stopped by another machine.[11]

This sequence of elimination of hands by increased use of automatic operation illustrates the distinction between mechanization (the whole) and automation (the part). Automation is on the growing edge of mechanization. For years, displacement of men and animals by machines has been a common phenomenon. Automation, the new economic fact of our day, is "the substitution of mechanical, hydraulic, pneumatic, electrical and electronic devices for human organs of observation, decision and effort, so as to increase productivity, control quality, and reduce costs." [12] Mechanization has always aimed at the reduction of human muscle effort and, as such, we have welcomed it. Automation moves beyond into the functions of observation and decision-making. Not only must we cope with the problem of human displacement; not only must we learn to live with the leisure created by an increase in automated productivity; now we must find a solution to the question of boredom and intellectual deterioration on the part of the few who will staff the automated factories.

As I write, the national unemployment figure is running close to 7 per cent of the labor force. This percentage is an aggregate figure representing all of those, fourteen years old or older, who are actively seeking paid work and are unable to find it. A variety of factors could be listed as causing this unemployment. Automation is not the only villain of this particular piece. Other forms of technological change, depleted resources, shifting markets, new patterns of consumption can all be said to influence the aggregate figure. Automation contributes to the ranks of the jobless in two ways: by displacement and by what is sometimes called "silent firing." Displacement occurs when a man is "bumped" by a machine into another job within the same plant or the same industry, or when he finds that change has passed him by and he is out of work. The victim of "silent firing," on the other hand, is not the worker who loses his job as a result of technological change, but rather the worker who is not hired as a result of technological change. The case of the automated office well illustrates this point. Management decides to substitute machines for hands in office and clerical work where labor turnover is often high as young women work a few years, marry, and soon drop out of the labor force. With the decision to automate, management also decides not to release present employees but to let the normal process of attrition run its course so that the desired reduction of personnel will take place under a policy of no-firing accompanied by a sister policy or no-hiring. The ethical obligation of management toward those it does not hire is hardly the same as it is toward those it may or may not fire. Most management people are aware of their ethical responsibilities toward those with whom they are linked by virtue of a wage contract. Far fewer businessmen, however, acknowledge any social obligation toward those who are displaced or unemployed elsewhere in the economy. Does the ethician wish to pin an obligation on the business community to bear the expense of retraining or relocating workers? If he does, then it would seem that this can only be done through legislation. I will return to this point and related questions shortly.

The ethician is not the only one with problems in the face of this distinction between the aggregate unemployment total and the lesser army of displaced workers. Not all the unemployed have been displaced by technological change. The economist, too, must keep this distinction in mind as he plans his policy recommendations. For instance, the economic judgment that tax benefits for new business investment will encourage economic growth and thus create new jobs is directed toward the aggregate unemployment problem and could quite conceivably be of no effect at all in helping displaced workers or assisting depressed local economies. Recall the changing geographic structure of American industry and consider whether or not a general liberalization of depreciation allowances is going to divert the flow of capital back into the depressed areas. I doubt that it will. I also doubt the validity of Senator Goldwater's judgment that a general tax cut for business would soon create "a manpower shortage in this country." [13]

When the economist recommends fiscal (government tax and spending) or monetary (credit) measures to check mounting unemployment, he would do us all a great service by accompanying his recommendations with a careful projection of their expected impact on particular classes of unemployed people and on specific places of chronic distress. Such an attempt would at least make evident the painful fact that tax breaks for business and the consumer, together with easy credit to stimulate borrowing for business expansion, are aimed at trimming the aggregate unemployment figure in the wake of a soaring Gross National Product. In terms of a solution for depressed areas, however, such measures could be quite ineffective. Specific proposals for depressed areas are needed.

Creation of the Area Redevelopment Administration was a top-priority piece of New Frontier legislation happily signed into law by President Kennedy on May 1, 1961. The President thus fulfilled a campaign promise to the people of West Virginia and Pennsylvania and concluded a long legislative battle which he had waged unsuccessfully as a Senator through several earlier sessions of Congress. I favor this program of loans and grants to depressed rural and industrial communities, but I also feel that it alone will not work. Companion programs of retraining and relocation are needed. Senator McCarthy would suggest something on the order of the Reconstruction Finance Corporation as a stronger and more effective means to get these communities on their feet. Something is certainly needed to spur the unwilling, unable, or unimaginative banks and businesses within the depressed areas. Both the new ARA and the old RFC could be helpful despite the fact that both suffer from built-in vulnerability to political trades and the ruthless pressures of special interest groups.

I place much confidence on a remedy from within the depressed areas themselves. I do not, however, hesitate at all to look to the federal government for measures that will make such remedies practicable. Government contracts would be part, but only a minor part, of such expected federal assistance. I think the following argument, put forward by the president of the Northeast Pennsylvania Industrial Development Commission in opposition to a proposed federal program for relocating idle workers, demonstrates a short-sighted attitude toward the possible help government can give and an unrealistic appraisal of communities where unemployment percentages have consistently run far above the national average for about fifteen years:

What the people of northeastern Pennsylvania's several surplus areas ask of the Federal Government is a realistic system of Federal installations and Federal contracts to take up the unemployment slack. We have the human resources, our fine people, and all of the community facilities, churches, schools, cultural activities, financial and government operations well established. If planners are to plan, let them plan to help us, not to develop some grandiose scheme that will relocate part of our population.[14]

It is a bit gratuitous to assert that the relocation of some surplus labor could only harm the depressed areas.

The recurring ethical question underlying this entire discussion was raised more than a decade ago by economist Fritz Machlup now of Princeton University. Professor Machlup wrote:

> Most of us have come to believe that the hardships of those who suffer from economic change should not be overlooked and that society, benefiting from the change, has a moral obligation to relieve distress and to facilitate adjustments, but not to resist the change and suppress innovation.[15]

Notice that the social obligation cuts both ways. Distress must be relieved and adjustments facilitated. Yet the means selected to achieve these ends must not be chosen with a view to suppressing genuine progress. Trouble arises when people who discuss this question come down too hard on the side of one obligation while ignoring the other. For instance, people in those depressed areas which have been stranded in the wake of technological change would like to think that the nation which has benefited from the change recognizes a moral obligation to relieve their distress and facilitate adjustment. They might expect unions and management to meet the expense of severance pay, retraining and some measure of unemployment compensation; they would also look to the nation as a whole for approval of tax expenditures for the relief of their distress. Their more affluent countrymen, however, wonder at times whether the rising unemployment barometer has effectively pushed aside resistance to change and innovation within these same depressed areas. Arguments from the prosperous parts of the country might try to urge an obligation upon displaced workers to relocate when work is available elsewhere, rather than remain at home entertaining uncertain hopes of better times to come.

One way of discharging the social obligation of relieving the distress of chronically unemployed is through retraining and relocation. The economic question is "retraining whom for what?" The "whom" calls for a careful consideration of class—younger workers (training and education will facilitate mobility among this class), older workers (over forty-five), the woman, the Negro. Certain background limitations will make any degree of genuine education impossible. Certain age categories, together with the inability to acquire skills, will make mobility unlikely. The "for what" is a much larger question. Where exactly are the new job opportunities going to be created in our economy? What precisely are the new skills that will be in demand? Are workers to be trained for jobs in the production of services, consumer goods, or capital goods?

The important ethical question is, "Who will pay the bill?" Is this a matter for individual initiative, for private enterprise? If it is, then I fear that the chronically unemployed will be forever idle. If society has a moral obligation, how does society proceed to discharge such an obligation? Granted that technological change is inevitable and must not be resisted. Granted that today's technological change may begin a revolution which in twenty years or so will yield a harvest of new products, new markets and new jobs. Still, who is content to wait for twenty years to see the worker who is displaced by today's technological change get back to work again? I think that taxes on business and personal income should provide the means to relieve distress and facilitate adjustment. I think that the federal government should assume primary responsibility for prompt and effective action in this regard. Specifically, the federal government should encourage, assist, and supplement private, local, and state efforts to train new workers and retrain displaced workers. Similar encouragement, assistance and supplementation should be given labor unions and industries in their efforts to facilitate the geographic mobility of displaced workers.

If the ethician is wondering how he can instruct particular individuals or groups in our society in their moral responsibility toward the displaced and unemployed, let him first get laws on the books and then remind men of their obligations under the law. Such obligations would range from nondiscriminatory hiring to giving adequate advance notice of planned lay-offs. If unions and management do nothing to provide severance pay for displaced workers, laws might be passed that would force them to provide this much of a cushion. Tax obligations must, of course, be emphasized by the ethician. I see no other way of attaining any meaningful level of social justice in the American environment of free enterprise, collective bargaining, due process and democratic government, than by first passing laws on the basis of which genuine social injustice can be declared illegal. The Supreme Court's famous desegregation decision of 1954 illustrated the path which America is following toward social justice. The question before us at the moment, however, is the handling of technological change without injustice toward men who have invested their energies, aspirations and perhaps most of their productive years in a job that no longer exists.

Benjamin M. Selekman would use the following fourfold norm to judge a corporation's ability to handle by itself the displacement consequent upon mechanization:

(1) Whether or not, and to what degree, management assumes responsibility for the human as well as the technical aspects.

(2) What the character of the labor force is.

(3) Whether it is a growth industry.

(4) Whether it enjoys a favorable position in its market.[16]

If norms (1), (3), or (4) turn up negative, to whose shoulders does the social obligation shift? I fail to see how government can stay or be kept out of this picture. This does not mean that there will be no room for private effort; private effort is necessary but it alone will not suffice. The American Telephone and Telegraph Company has displayed considerable responsibility in this regard; so has Armour and Company which is attacking the displacement problem in a joint effort with the United Packinghouse Workers and the Amalgamated Meat Cutters Union. The International Longshoremen's and Warehousemen's Union signed an agreement with the Pacific Maritime Association in October, 1960 giving the employers greater freedom to mechanize and modernize in exchange for a fund which will total $33,500,000 by 1966 and which the union will administer in providing retraining, early retirement and other benefits to the men who are displaced by mechanization. If more employers and unions were both willing and able to assume responsibility in this matter, the need for government activity would be less urgent.

The United States Employment Service might be able to encourage labor mobility by bringing knowledge of job opportunities to the chronically unemployed. This could be done by gathering and transmitting information from local and state agencies around the country. Automation may be the key in providing quick and accurate information as a basis for easier mobility of both labor and capital. This could be done by wider use of computers and "intellectronic" supervision of the movement of resources in our economy.

Policy recommendations from outside the depressed areas often favor a combination of retraining and relocation for the relief of chronic unemployment. Economic forces should be able to pull labor from where it is idle to where it is needed—so runs the argument. Within the depressed areas, retraining is welcomed but, as has already been indicated, relocation is almost always viewed with suspicion and even hostility by official spokesmen. When the Kennedy Administration declared its interest in relocation proposals, one newspaper in a depressed Pennsylvania community said flatly: "The relocation move is certainly not wanted in areas such as this which already have been hit by population losses." Another paper in the same state took a different viewpoint in arguing against the same proposal:

For some years we have had to resign ourselves to the flight from their home communities of our youth, high school and college graduates, forced to go to other parts of the country to find jobs and to lay the basis for their careers. This is an experience known to many families here.

It accordingly seems a little too much to ask now that on top of the loss of our young people we agree to permit our older residents, who have their roots firmly established here, to be shifted to other parts of the nation on the chance that they will find jobs elsewhere. The fact that we would in the process suffer a further loss of population is not too important, but the humane considerations involved in such a dislocation are great.

The editorial fails to take into account that relocations would be voluntary; only those who had assurance of employment elsewhere would qualify, and only those who had been out of work for many months would be considered. Further, when the Administration's thought in this regard was articulated by the Secretary of Labor before the Subcommittee on Employment and Manpower of the Senate Committee on Labor and Public Welfare,[17] it became clear that the program would affect only about three thousand workers annually with the government meeting only 50 per cent of the cost of relocation. Presumably, the worker's willingness to be "uprooted" would be demonstrated by his acceptance of 50 per cent of the cost.

At any rate, when the Committee on Labor and Public Welfare reported out the Manpower Development and Training Act of 1961 (S. 1991, introduced by Senator Joseph S. Clark [D.—Pa.]), the bill's original proposal for relocation allowances was deleted, making the legislation principally a training and retraining measure. As thus amended, the bill passed the Senate and was sent to the House where it will be neither debated nor voted on before this First Session of the Eighty-seventh Congress adjourns. And when Congress adjourns, the number of idle workers who have been out of work for more than six consecutive months will be still around the one million mark! [18]

I think that a program of retraining and relocation is both good economics and in the best interest of the individuals most immediately affected by chronic unemployment. The idle mills, mines and shops of our nation's depressed areas are not only mute witnesses to past prosperity and economic change but they also testify to the absence of intelligent, long-range planning by leaders in the distressed communities.[19] It seems to me that indispensable elements of any sensible, long-term, economic rehabilitation program for the depressed areas would be regional planning and out-migration of some of the unemployed, combined with local efforts to create new businesses and attract new industries from outside.

Regional planning begins by working toward the abandonment of obsolete, "horse-and-buggy," local, governmental jurisdictions in favor of governmental units that are metro-wide or wider, vested with economic and political power for effective overall government. While regional government cannot be achieved overnight, it is a goal well worth reaching for today by leaders in neighboring towns and communities which suffer together from economic blight. Simultaneously, community cooperation should be encouraged in the matter of finding new job opportunities for the unemployed. This calls for realistic planning with regard to mobility of both labor and capital. Some idle workers should be retrained with an eye to relocation. Others should be retrained to form a pool of skilled labor at home as an attraction to new industry. But depressed areas should not be too hopeful about their chances to win new industries from outside. Another look at the changing geography of American industry should caution them against undue optimism in the treasure hunt for new industry. High sounding adjectives will not shift the tide of industrial migration back to the areas where unemployment is chronic. Some new locations will be won by depressed areas but many more new jobs will be needed. On the principle that most new business is native to the area where it appears, local industrial developers should do more to ferret out local ideas which show promise of producing home-grown industries.[20]

Characteristically, the depressed areas are unable to prevent their youths from leaving in search of better economic opportunities elsewhere. This loss of mental capital can be reduced if community leaders help the young to capitalize marketable ideas which display employment potential. Many Chamber of Commerce people are so busy polishing up the civic image that they ignore the possibility of finding very close to home a machinist, mechanic, technician, or merchant who has an idea that could be converted into jobs. Generous development credit arrangements will be needed to get new ventures going or to enlarge old ones. In the more urbanized depressed areas, local professional associations should provide graduate fellowships in medicine, accounting, law, business management, industrial relations, journalism, public administration and engineering, all with a string attached that would pull the fellow home to begin his professional career and thus keep the local professions and businesses in vital contact with growing ideas and new methods.

I hope it is clear from the preceding pages that "class" and "mass" unemployment call for different remedies; that the problem of unemployment and the problem of chronic unemployment are not the same. The aggregate unemployment figure can be effectively reduced by vigorous private enterprise in a growth economy. In the matter of chronic unemployment, however, private enterprise has failed to meet the challenge. New experiments—private and public—are needed.

The ethician will agree that there is a moral imperative to do *something*. He will rely on a prudential legislative judgment to endow that "something" with the binding force of law. The legislator, in turn, will look to the economist who will best serve the public good by using all his skill and knowledge to define clearly the framework within which the problem of chronic unemployment can be solved.

NOTES

1. *Economic Intelligence,* Vol. XIII, No. 6 (June, 1960), p. 1.
2. U. S. Senate, *Report of the Special Committee on Unemployment Problems,* Report No. 1206, Eighty-sixth Congress, 2nd Session (Washington, D. C.: Government Printing Office, 1960), p. 122.
3. *Ibid.,* p. 72.
4. See U. S. Department of Labor, *Manpower, Challenge of the 1960s*

(Washington, D. C.: Government Printing Office, 1960). This report is discussed by Seymour L. Wolfbein, Deputy Assistant Secretary of Labor, on pp. 27-36 of this book.

5. See Harold L. Sheppard, Louis A. Ferman, and Seymour Faber, "Too Old to Work—Too Young to Retire: A Case Study of a Permanent Plant Shutdown," Committee Print issued by the Special Committee on Unemployment Problems, U. S. Senate, Eighty-sixth Congress, 1st Session (Washington, D. C.: Government Printing Office, 1960).

6. See Walter Isard and Victor Fuchs, "Is American Industry Moving to New Locations?" A paper delivered at the Conference on the Changing Character of American Industry, sponsored by the AFL-CIO, January 18, 1958, and printed in *The Changing Character of American Industry* (Washington, D. C.: AFL-CIO, 1958), Publication No. 67, pp. 51-68.

7. *Report of the Special Senate Committee on Unemployment Problems, op. cit.*, p. 44.

8. *Ibid.*, p. 46.

9. Statement appearing in *New Views of Automation*. Papers submitted to the Subcommittee on Automation and Energy Resources, Joint Economic Committee, Congress of the United States (Washington, D. C.: Government Printing Office, 1960), pp. 49-75. See also Dr. Buckingham's book, *Automation: Its Impact on Business and People* (New York: Harper, 1961).

10. *Ibid.*, p. 62.

11. As men are replaced by machines, the individual worker will feel pressures driving him toward slowdowns and various forms of work sabotage. The ethical procedure to be expected in such circumstances is to accept the conditions and meet the requirements agreed upon through collective bargaining.

12. This is the definition of automation formulated by the First International Automation Exposition, held in New York in November, 1954. The definition is quoted by Clyde E. Dankert, "Automation and Unemployment," *Studies in Unemployment* (Washington, D. C.: Government Printing Office, 1960), p. 225.

13. See Senator Goldwater's remarks on *A Conservative Views Automation* on p. 190 of this book.

14. Press Release, Hazelton, Pa., May 23, 1961, reprinted in the *Congressional Record*, May 29, 1961, and entered as testimony in Hearings on the Training of the Unemployed, Subcommittee on Employment and Manpower, U. S. Senate, March 20, 1961, p. 13.

15. *The Basing Point System* (Philadelphia: The Blakiston Co., 1949), p. 269.

16. "Businessmen in Power," *Harvard Business Review*, Vol. 39, No. 5 (September-October, 1961), p. 106.

17. See *Hearings on the Training of the Unemployed, op. cit.*, p. 235.

18. The bill was passed in the Second Session of the Eighty-seventh Congress.—Editor's note.

19. As long ago as 1914, the City of Scranton, Pennsylvania, formed an industrial development company and issued a prospectus which had the ring of prophecy but suffered the fate of a prophet in his home country: "The mining of coal is not a permanent industry. Each day sees the city nearer the time when this business will have passed entirely away so far as our participation in it is concerned. Fortunately for us this change will be gradual, and we shall not suffer any violent economic overturn. The situation which confronts us, however, is a concrete industrial problem which must be met and solved if we are to endure as a city."

20. I have discussed this problem at greater length in "Needed: Local Leadership in Depressed Areas," *Harvard Business Review*, Vol. 38, No. 4 (July-August, 1960), pp. 115-24.

CHAPTER 7

AUTOMATION
AND THE OLDER WORKER

by JAMES C. O'BRIEN, *Executive Director*
of the Committee on Older and Retired
Workers, United Steelworkers of America

IN THE LONG RUN, the blessings of automation are likely to eliminate the sources of hunger, scarcity, and poverty all over the world. What opportunities for life's fulfillment could flow from such developments!

However, if scarcity is replaced by plenty, there will be many changes in relationships between peoples, in ownership and property, government and freedom: i.e., the whole broad range of social concepts and relationships. It should be understood at the outset that the prospects of plenty at any time in the future depend on the continued absence of atomic war.

Any realistic appraisal of the impact of automation must recognize that life no longer burdened with scarcity of food, clothing, shelter, and other necessities and luxuries will be a different way of life, but one with a complete new range of problems. But before we reach that condition of having eliminated hunger and poverty—the veritable Garden of Eden—we will have to solve numerous and major problems on the way. In the imperfect manner by which we reach ultimate goals, some of the means to those ends are likely to present even bigger and more critical problems than we have now.

The path to abundance will be strewn with numerous economic dislocations even with dedication to care and planning, but at least these problems can be minimized. In the short run, while the benefits of automation are accruing to certain firms, their owners, and some of their employees, others will be forced out of business, their owners perhaps bankrupted and many workers unemployed and dependent on society for their survival. Much of this burden will fall on those who through no fault of their own become the economic victims of automation's progress.

The short range problems resulting from automation relate primarily to finding new sources of livelihood for those whose jobs have been automated out of existence and who are not able to obtain new jobs quickly and without undue personal suffering. In justice to the broad principles of humanity, we cannot ask a portion of our population to accept the economic burden of automation's short-range impacts (which may already be long-range, as indicated by official data showing that about 1,000,000 people [913,000] as of July, 1961 had been unemployed for 27 weeks or more, or in other words, more than 6 months) while the rest of our population accepts automation's bounty. While our whole society will have problems to solve, the major area of consideration in this paper will be on the particular implications of automation on employment and labor force problems as related to the older worker.

There are many definitions of automation and I think it is not necessary to dwell upon a precise meaning. Some people have suggested even that automation had its beginnings in the caveman's club. Broadly speaking, I would accept the definition of automation as the mechanization of thought, sensory, and control processes. Equally meaningful is the brief definition given by the Department of Labor to automation as the partial or full replacement of workers as a source of energy and/or control by machines.

Automation, in recent years, has tended to take on a new meaning. We are no longer talking about production methods which differ only in degree from those of the past, but of those which differ in kind. Today we do not think in terms of man having a machine available which he can run and attend to while the back-breaking, life-robbing physical exertions are eliminated, but of machines that run machines (by tape, numerical controls, and computers), which tend to outmode the necessity for man's employment altogether. This developing phenomenon might quickly be put aside from serious consideration as a meaningless irritant to our system, were it not for the many examples which are becoming more abundant—some of which I will cite—which are replacing men by the scores, hundreds, and thousands, nearly all of whom, under our organization of the economy, need other jobs or other sources of income to survive. Members of our own union, the Steelworkers, are among those which have seen their jobs disappear by the thousands as the new technology advances.

Let us look at some of the recent headline news on developments in automation. Recent reports show that next year at least 325,000 factory workers, or 2 per cent of the 16,000,000 people employed in manufacturing will lose their jobs because of newly installed labor saving devices. It is estimated that other fields will eliminate at least twice as many jobs because of automation next year as will manufacturing, bringing the total up to about 1,000,000. In 10 years, manufacturing employment could fall roughly about 20 per cent based on a 2 per cent reduction a year, or about 3,200,000. Add twice this number from other fields and the total displaced would be 9,600,-

000. The implications of the size of the employment problem which we face becomes clearer if we add to these 9,600,000 industrially displaced workers the 26,000,000 for whom new jobs will have to be found as they first enter the work force in the 1960s and another 3,000,000 for people returning to the labor force (such as housewives whose children no longer require their presence at home). We are talking then in terms of supplying between 35,000,000 to 40,000,000 new jobs within 10 years in an economy which now employs only about 68,000,000 and which has had about 7 per cent of its labor force unemployed for many months and many of these people unemployed for over 6 months already. These millions of new jobs will be needed in an era of ever-increasing productive efficiency not only in this country but abroad as well.

Evidence is mounting that other highly industrialized countries may soon face similar problems. In France, for example, Renault has increased its output by 600 per cent with an increase of only 40 per cent in its work force in the past 13 years; Sweden's S. K. F., a ball bearing manufacturer, tripled its prewar production with *no* increase in its labor force. Since 1953, manufacturing productivity has increased about 70 per cent in Japan and slightly over 50 per cent in both France and West Germany.

Now let me cite a few examples of recent developments in automation in this country, illustrative in different ways of what is and has been happening. Among the most dramatic is the new mill opened by Continental Copper and Steel Industries in Linden, New Jersey early in June, 1961. The plant cost $3,000,000 and turns out 200 miles of copper rod in an 8-hour day. How many employees are required in the operation of this plant? The answer is three (3)!

In steel, a new type LD oxygen process converter now

90

in operation is capable of and does produce 100 tons of steel in 25 minutes. It replaced an open hearth process that required 8 hours to produce the same amount of steel.

The long term trends in steel portray the steelworker's employment problems vividly. From 1937 through 1960, steel ingot production and finished steel shipments increased 75 per cent and 85 per cent respectively, in spite of a 10 per cent decline in employment from 512,900 in 1937 to 461,800 in 1960. Productivity in steel has thus been estimated to have increased 111 per cent in the span of those years. For the future, the employment outlook in steel is equally dim. Experts predict that productivity growth will approximate the increase in steel production and shipments throughout the sixties, so that at best we can expect only a small increase in employment from the 1960 average of 461,800 to about 500,000. But even at 500,000, the total will still be far below the 571,600 employed in the peak year of 1953. This small increase in the 1960s is of course predicated on no further breakthroughs in steel technology and, I would say, is based on relatively optimistic projections in regard to employment opportunities in the industry.

White collar workers are by no means exempt from the impact of automation. For example, it is estimated that 10,000 computer installations will be made in 1961. Each computer is likely to displace 35 workers permanently, or a total of 350,000 in 1961 alone. In the next 5 years, indications are that about 4,000,000 office and clerical jobs will be eliminated by automation. Conservative estimates indicate that annual expenditures for electronic data processing installations will amount to $2,000,000,000 in 1970, compared to $500,000,000 in 1961 and only to $10,000,000 in 1950. When phonetic typewriters, now being developed, are perfected, the jobs of 1,500,000 secretaries, stenographers and typists are likely to be eliminated permanently, or about the same number as the total currently employed in those occupations. A concrete example of automation's impact among clerical workers is found in the recent New York Stock Exchange announcement that upon installation of two new computing systems to spread the collection and transmission of price quotations to the daily newspapers, 40 tabulating employees will be displaced. The investment in these machines will amount to about $620,000 if purchased outright, or, if rented, will cost approximately $16,000 a month.

With these examples in mind, let us look for a moment at several management statements on the subject of whether automation will cause serious unemployment. J. J. Jaeger, a Pratt and Whitney executive, summarized the then dominant business and industrial attitude in a Fortune-sponsored symposium by stating: "These things take care of themselves . . . I don't think it is the part, nor can it be the part of industry to try to plan the social aspects of this thing." The National Association of Manufacturers, in the pamphlet, *Calling All Jobs,* rhapsodized:

> Let the worker face what is to come with hope in his heart, not with fear in his mind. Automation is a magical key to creation, not a blunt instrument of destruction, and the worker's talent and skill will continue to merit reward in the fairyland of the world to come.

Given the events of the past few years and the current facts in regard to unemployment, especially among the long-term unemployed, it is obvious that these two statements were unduly optimistic. The facts show that we are in desperate need of realistic planning among the nation's top experts in industry, labor, government, and the public to help offset the upheavals caused by automation.

The dimensions of the problem which we face in providing jobs for the available labor force were spelled out by economist Gabriel Kolko. The following analysis is based on the general methodology used by Kolko.

I have suggested that almost 10,000,000 workers will be replaced by automation in the next ten years and another 29,000,000 people will be entering or reentering the labor force and looking for jobs in this same period. Given the need for an investment of $20,000 in plant and equipment to provide one new job, it would require $200,000,-000,000 to provide jobs for automation's victims alone and another $580,000,000,000 for new and returning entrants into the labor force, or a total of $780,000,000,000 in the next 10 years!

Is it reasonable to assume that such tremendous investment funds will be forthcoming? The data available show that we have been investing $34,000,000,000 on plant and equipment on the average for the past 5 years. Continuation of this average over the next 10 years would amount to a total of $340,000,000,000 or considerably less than half of the $780,000,000,000 needed! If as much as $100,-000 were required per job (which is not even a maximum figure), the size of the investment needed to employ the millions of job seekers of the next 10 years becomes astronomically high. To conceive of investments of this magnitude flowing from our normal economic activity is sheer "fairyland" thinking.

Now let us consider the impact of all these changes brought about by automation as they affect the older worker.

Our attitudes and ideas often lag behind events, and the nostalgia that colors much American thinking prevents us from facing up to realities. As Senator Joseph Clark of Pennsylvania, among others, has repeatedly pointed out, our problems are those of an urbanized society. The metropolis, or city, has already become dominant as a place where most Americans live. However, our love of the past and the exalted view of the value of a rural America have inhibited efforts to reorganize our political and social thinking and structure of government to cope with the problems of our cities and people who live in them.

The 20,000,000 people associated with farming received $5,900,000,000 from the Federal Treasury in 1960, or an average payment of $1,160 in cash per farm family.

I am for an intelligent farm program and assistance to this important segment of our national economy. I feel, however, that it is all too true that Senator Clark meets with a good deal of indifference in his efforts to get Americans to think in terms of contemporary realities rather than with concepts outmoded by the dynamic events of the last 50 years. Unfortunately, there is great opposition to even limited Federal expenditures for conservation of our urban resources.

I touched on the problems of the cities and the difference in the approach to city problems and farm problems because I think this paralleled the trends in thinking that we encounter when we contemplate the problems of the older worker in industrial society or, as the title of this session has it, "business society."

First of all, a largely agricultural, small town America of a half-century or more ago seemed better able to accommodate the aged and aging. There was plenty of work on the farms, light enough for those who were physically less able. Large homes and large families insulated them against the uncertainties of their later years. Though probably it was nowhere near as satisfactory as some sentimentalists would have it, there was, nevertheless, a way within the framework of the times to satisfy the social needs.

It goes without saying that we have witnessed the disappearance of more and more family operated farms, and small homes and apartments have become the order of the day. The population has shifted to urban and suburban areas.

Accompanying all the swift changes has been a very fundamental one in the manner in which Americans are enabled to provide for themselves the necessities of life as well as many of its comforts. The area of production is rarely now the area of consumption. The Jeffersonian hopes of a nation of small freeholders, who, through ownership of property (in this case, land), would be the bulwark of democracy and political freedom has lost significance except in the pamphlets of the Dixiecrats.

We are more and more a centralized, urbanized, industrialized, mass market, typified by a mass producing, mass media, mass consuming society. For better or for worse, it is within this context that our problems must be solved.

I would imagine that, with few exceptions, all of us participating in this discussion are dependent on wages or salary for all that we have in the way of a standard of living. I would further guess that for those who would claim ownership, it is of property such as a home rather than productive property, and even here we find that a bank, with a thirty-year mortgage, owns more of our house, or the finance company, more of our car, than we do. And, if you own stock, it is hard to get a feeling, such as possession of a farm once gave, that you are a real owner of General Motors or A.T.&.T. In any event, your stock ownership is effectively divorced from control whereas the property philosophy of our forefathers embraced the idea of ownership being all important because it permitted control.

In his new book, *Power without Property,* Adolf Berle re-emphasizes a lesson he has been trying to get across for years. That is, that in spite of anti-trust activity, the Sherman and Clayton Acts, and the Federal Trade Commission, the American corporate system now represents the highest concentration of economic power in recorded history. And it is as a person without property in the traditional sense that the older worker takes his place in this economic complex as a very small drop in a vast business sea and depends on government and unions (to a large degree the younger worker does, too) to help him achieve status.

Again though, the myths haunt us. There was, of course, a time even in the early stage of industrialization that, except for the periodic depressions, there were jobs available in any expanding and rapidly growing manufacturing system. Men could migrate from job shortage areas to job surplus areas with reasonable expectations of obtaining employment, whether they were young or old. This, and the tradition of the frontier and free land in the West, are responsible for many present misconceptions. There have not been, except in World War II, any real labor shortages for 30 years. Even now, only the cold war and the millions of jobs created by our $43,000,000,000 defense expenditure disguise the real dimension of the problem. It is fortunate that we are recovering from the recent recessions, even though unemployment remains at unconscionably high levels. The waste inherent in any recession, in terms of national needs and human suffering, can scarcely be exaggerated. Of course, in each of these recessions, older workers are laid off who are never recalled to their jobs and they are added to the payment pool of unemployed or take jobs at levels far below their normal skills and achievements, and generally at much lower pay.

Now I am aware that through the great social legislation of the New Deal and the contracts negotiated by labor unions, much has been accomplished. It is true that much of what has been achieved by the unions has found its way into general practice in the unorganized sector of the work force. However, unemployment compensation and social security, union seniority rights, and supplementary unemployment benefits still leave many areas of need untouched.

Now I want to turn your attention again to my previous comments on property. Mr. Berle remains optimistic about the ability of Americans to find a way to continue to solve the problems of capitalism without falling victim to the predictions of Karl Marx. He feels we have evolved a system already vastly superior to either communism or traditional capitalism and that we have done so without realizing it. I am perhaps not so certain as he that we have really found answers to the basic problems, but I am hopeful.

When you have, through the years, developed a method by which millions of workers accrue greater security in the job through seniority, you are certainly making progress. When you create pension plans and later improve and liberalize them, you are certainly advancing social good. While these things have often been done piecemeal, I think that they advance the notion of the real possibility of society's ultimate recognition that there is, in effect, a property right in a job and that this right increases with years of service; that it cannot lightly be taken away and certainly not unilaterally. If, and I must be frank here, some elements of business find this offensive, I can only point out that unfortunately they felt the same way about paid vacations, holidays, sick leave, and insurance, not to mention the violent battle they fought against pension and supplementary unemployment benefits. In any event, it seems to me that external forces that cannot really be overcome force us more and more in this direction, and that commerce and industry will have to accept it as a social if not an economic necessity.

Let us take this a step further now, if you will consent to my presuming that there will be wide public acceptance, backed by legislation and contract, of the thesis that a job is property.

The headlines of the day from Cuba remind us that property is often expropriated as a matter of public policy. There are few who would argue that governments have no right to do this but only that there must be grave need, just cause, and adequate compensation. Whether there will be a fair return for the lands confiscated in Cuba is uncertain, but when we use the right of eminent domain for slum clearance, highway building, and power projects in this country, the essential need to give relief commensurate with the loss is recognized.

Now, the efficiency of business and industry is important to a society based on free enterprise. The advancements and improvements brought about by technological change are necessary and in the long run beneficial. There can be little doubt that, by and large, individual needs must give way to social necessity. However, if a worker is to be replaced through automation or by a new process, is he not entitled to receive as a matter of public policy the recognition that his property right in his job is to be adequately compensated for through norms of justice which we have yet to work out? Of course, the worth of this property interest in the job would vary with his years of service and would not be the same for the man with five years as for the one with twenty-five.

Let me illustrate this. If in a large steel, auto, or rubber plant the introduction of a computer system and control devices eliminates the need for a man who at age fifty has accumulated thirty years of service, we have a real problem on our hands. I repeat my assertion to the McNamara Committee that he may very well be an industrial displaced person. The techniques and special accomplishments which he had gained through his long years of employment are likely to be of little or no value elsewhere and even if they were, his chances of being hired at age fifty or better are close to nil in most companies today.

Apropos of this, Senator McCarthy's Committee on Unemployment which held hearings in Pittsburgh, Pennsylvania, in 1960, had one witness appear who, at age thirty-three, had been turned down in the few plants that were hiring because they were engaging only men between eighteen and thirty.

To repeat what I said earlier, if work is available at all to men over forty, it is largely marginal and at subsistence wages or less, and will not provide a living for a man and his dependents on reasonable standards of health and decency. What then is to be done for these hundreds of thousands of older workers with the desire and the need to hold jobs? What is to be the recognition of the twenty-five, thirty, and forty years of investment of mental and physical effort that constituted his capital and which was every bit as important as the money needed for the business enterprise? If my conviction that his job, as his property, has been confiscated by the requirements of the system is correct, then the following possibilities for labor-management cooperation open up:

(1) That all reasonable attempts will be made to plan ahead for such contingencies and the earliest possible warning given the union and the industrial worker.

(2) That there will be a priority claim on any possible opening elsewhere in the enterprise and a transfer of his property rights to a job there.

(3) That management, first on a company level, and then on an industry-wide basis, will attempt to have

99

a coordinated system for exchange of information and rapid communication of employment data. Then, that arrangements will be worked out whereby the costs of the movement of the worker and his family to other plants within the company and other companies within the industry will be absorbed as a part of the cost of doing business.

(4) That for those for whom no work exists in their fields, a continually replenished reserve, built from the savings of automation, will be maintained. From this reserve, the necessary moneys will be provided for vocational rehabilitation of workers when their jobs have become obsolete.

(5) Pension rights, after a reasonable minimum time, will be transferable to make mobility more attractive and prevent the loss of much-needed security for old age.

(6) Obsolete and unnecessary rules discriminating in hiring on the basis of age will be discarded.

(7) Supplementary benefits and severance pay will be improved to reduce the sudden impact of catastrophic personal crisis on an older worker and his family due to unemployment.

(8) Labor and management will work jointly to find sound and constructive legislative programs for presentation at the state and federal level to handle those problems so broad in scope that they are beyond the best efforts of private groups.

Since business has objected traditionally to government intervention in the socio-economic sphere through its organized spokesmen and associations, there presents itself to the business community a splendid opportunity for

100

intelligent and voluntary action in cooperation with labor. This joint endeavor to tackle a mutual problem of older worker needs can bring great dividends to both.

The National Industrial Conference Board (a business research group) released figures compiled by a panel of economists in New York on November 22, 1959. They claimed that the phenomenal growth rate of the United States in the past hundred years had slowed in the 1950s until we stood at the bottom of industrial nations, not the least of which is Soviet Russia. Martin Gainsbrugh, chief economist of the Board, blames this largely on our increased leisure. Certainly, much of the leisure forced upon the older worker is as unwelcome as it is unsought. If we truly wish to raise the economic growth rate of the country, it seems unreasonable that we would leave untapped these vast reserves of producers and consumers who are now undervalued, underutilized and, I am afraid, often undernourished. There is great need for all of us—labor, management, government and community groups—to launch effective programs immediately.

The greatest challenge confronting the business community is the 16,000,000 people presently over 65, 3 out of 5 of whom have less than $1,000 per year to live on. There are also about 10,000,000 people working who do not have a minimum wage of $1.00 per hour with the dollar worth less than 50 cents in terms of purchasing power today.

Add to this frightening figure at least 4,500,000 unemployed and we have almost 30,000,000 people trying to live on a bare subsistence income at a time when we boast of our great prosperity and when, through automation and advanced technology, our capacity to produce is constantly and dramatically increasing.

Contrast this situation with that of Russia where significant advances are being made in living standards—

where it is claimed there is no unemployment, with health and medical care provided for all the people—and then the magnitude of the challenge becomes readily apparent.

Recognition of this problem in the midst of increasing productivity makes clear the need for management and labor to join forces with other elements in the community in order to find a humane and constructive solution to the problem of meeting the legitimate needs of at least one-sixth of our population.

CHAPTER 8

AUTOMATION AND MANAGEMENT DECISIONS

by REV. THOMAS M. GARRETT, S.J.,
Professor of Philosophy, University of Scranton

IN THE POPULAR IMAGINATION, automation is generally associated with industry. Yet there is probably more automation in the office than in the factory.[1] Indeed, as the rising cost of clerical work creates a demand for cheaper methods of doing routine tasks, the office will come to be the real home of automation. Perhaps it might be better to say that that such automation as Computer Process Control will make the office and the factory into a single system whose heart will be located near the desks of top management. Now that computers can handle payrolls, accounting, market research, budget and operating forecasts, production and scheduling, we can expect them to have a greater and greater role in decision-making at the very highest levels. As a result, we may also expect the most serious ethical problems connected with automation to be found, not in the foundry or in a cracking plant, but in the executive board room.

As yet we do not have enough information to warrant any definite statement as to the actual effects of computers on executive decisions. Moreover, what we know of the effects of automation on factory workers shows how risky it is to make *a priori* judgments. For all this, it is possible to speak of the problems that may arise. What we know of the nature and limits of the machines as well as of the outlook of those who design and use them are highly suggestive as to the possible dangers and ethical problems which may arise.

These ethical problems have not escaped the leaders in this field,[2] and the moralist ought to be aware of at least the general areas where problems can occur. If nothing else, the awareness may stimulate him to study the question more deeply. Indeed, since many of the problems raised by the use of computers in executive decision-making are only one aspect of more general problems concerned with the use of scientific method and scientific data, such a study can also serve as an introduction to a whole field of morality which has hardly been explored in any depth.

The Machines

At the very start it will be useful to recall a few fundamental facts about the modern calculating machines.[3] Essentially, these machines record numbers, operate with numbers, and give results in numerical form. Some of them, of course, have receptors which enable them to get new information, memories which store it and even a sort of nervous system which enables the calculator to check its own operations. For all this, they remain in the last analysis machines which deal with numbers, or at very least, with the quantified expression of relationships.

In the case of digital computers,[3] as opposed to analogue machines, the data is represented as a set of choices among a number of contingencies. The accuracy of the machine depends quite obviously upon the sharpness with which the contingencies have been distinguished, the number of alternatives presented in every choice, and the number of choices given. Most digital machines are based on a system of binary choices; that is, on questions which can be answered by a *yes* or a *no*.

Now these few simple statements point up two important limitations of the calculators. First, they can only handle matters which can be coded mathematically without significant deformation of the data. Secondly, the ordinary computer can only handle questions which can be answered by a *yes* or a *no*. Of course, one could use a trinary system which provided for a "don't know" reply, but this would involve the use of a special logic.

To understand the real significance of these two limitations we must recall the fact that the construction, programming and use of the machines involve simplifications even when the data can be treated numerically. Further, the human element enters in at most of the decisive moments in the total process. Thus, men choose the goals which the machine is to attain. At best, the machine is like a pilot who receives his orders from the captain of the ship and then relays them to the engine room and to the steersman. If the goal has been improperly chosen, carelessly defined or even changed, the machine will grind out its answers which, though they may be logical in terms of the instructions given it, may be at odds with the actual purpose of the captain. The machine, in other words, can be like the logical paranoiac who is perfectly consistent with his premises, but completely out of contact with the real world.

The captain, moreover, must give his orders in a language which is intelligible to the machine and decide what factors it is to consider in guiding the ship to its port. This involves a double simplification. In the first place, since the machine speaks in numbers and since mathematical formulae are not exact reproductions of reality, something is lost in the process of translation. This may be of little importance when you are dealing with physical realities, but could represent a real deformation when a man's personality is reduced to a series of index numbers preliminary to calculating his suitability for a job.

The simplification involved in selecting factors for translation is perhaps more significant, and especially so when there is a question of immaterial reality. Suppose, for example, the machine is to be used in selecting executives. Emotional balance, motivation, initiative, intelligence, skill, vision, and general character cannot be measured directly. Consequently, those who make up the program for the machine select certain material signs which are generally, but not necessarily, associated with various qualities. These are then given a numerical weight and fitted to an equation. These last two steps involve more than one set of assumptions for there were simplifications in the original statistical work which set up the correlations and in the psychological theory which lay behind the studies. Finally, the equation itself is liable to be selected on the basis of its ability to give results in accord with theory rather than on a basis of proven correspondence.[4]

In practice, of course, the computers do not consider all factors. Though the machine can work faster than a man, it still has a limited capacity with the result that only the more significant data is used. What needs to be remembered is the fact that such simplification means you are dealing not with certainties but with probabilities. Since these apply to groups and not to individuals, great care must be taken when using the answers supplied by the calculator in judging an individual case.

The Ethical Problems

Even these few simple ideas about the calculating machines give some idea of the sort of ethical problem which can arise when they are used to make decisions affecting human beings. First, if the goal is not in accord with sound ethics, the machine will give an answer which, while it is technically correct, may be humanly monstrous. Furthermore, if the man who uses the data from the machine is not aware of the goal, which is a sort of criterion, he may apply conclusions without realizing that they are not relevant to the end he has in mind. Dr. Norbert Wiener pointed this out when he wrote:

> If the rules for victory in a war game do not correspond to what we actually wish for our country, it is more likely that such a machine may produce a policy that will win a nominal victory on points at the cost of every interest we have at heart, even that of national survival.[5]

One might add that it is not merely a question of the rules corresponding to our wishes, but also to our obligations and duties, whether in war or business. Indeed, since the machines operate automatically once started, their use makes it imperative that the designers, programmers, and users be grounded in ethics.

Equally important is the fact that the machines may give a pseudo rationality to decisions precisely because they answer with a clear *yes* or *no* even to questions that permit of no such reply. Indeed, if the alternatives have not been carefully selected *and tested for ethical quality and human relevance,* the answers may be not only incomplete, but dangerous even in those areas where a *yes* or *no* answer might be legitimately given. This means that both the programmer and the user of the computer must have a wide knowledge of alternatives and a good deal of skill

107

in evaluating their ethical value. A few illustrations will help to clarify this point.

Let us suppose that the programmer and designer do not include social costs in their calculations of profitability. They are, of course, liable to do this since most economic theory makes no allowances for such factors. With such factors omitted from the program, the answer may be correct from the narrow viewpoint of the firm and immoral from the social standpoint. If the executive who uses the results is aware of the omission, he can adjust for it. If, however, he has no knowledge of this point, he may feel justified in acting on the basis of the reports he has been given. Similarly, if the program for executive selection omits, as it almost necessarily must, such qualities as sense of social responsibility and vision, it may recommend men who are both narrow and ruthless. Again, adjustments can be made, but these will depend on the awareness of what did and did not go into the computer in the first place.

All of this comes down to saying that the results given by a data processing machine are no better than the social ethics, economic and psychological theory which lay behind its construction.[6] This does not mean that the machines are any more prone to error than the executive operating in the ordinary way. As a matter of fact, the machine can actually give superior results in some cases. The danger arises from the fact that admiration for the technician, or ignorance of the machine's limits can lead to a neglect of the ethical factors. To put it another way, a naive faith in the omniscience of the calculator may be an excuse for irresponsible decision-making.

This is not merely the reaction of a naive ethician. Several authors have noted that management has not only been fascinated but also intimidated by the extreme complexity of automation. In some cases, it has allowed the

108

technicians to take over not only the operation of the machines, but also the management decisions as to how they are to be used. Others have noted a tendency on the part of some executives to buy high priced scientific services to use as excuses in the event of failure. Even aside from such obvious errors, we must face the fact that as automation increases, the influence of the engineers will rise.[7] Given the fact that technicians are more interested in efficiency than in human values, there is a danger that spiritual values and truly human goals may be relegated to second place. To put it another way, the combination of executive ignorance or irresponsibility and engineering rationality may produce a climate of decision which is basically amoral.

Though I am not one of those who live in fear that the machines will take over the world, we must not miss the fact that the very decision to use them in human areas poses problems. Because I must select factors which can be expressed mathematically, I am tempted to omit those which will not fit my requirements, and to distort others in an effort to make them fit. In other words, the need for quantification may lead to stripping off the non-quantifiable layers of reality and to reducing man to a cipher. The demands of the machine can thus recreate the creator to the image and likeness of his creature.

While this last point may seem extreme, those who have had even a little experience with such relatively simple machines as those used to work out college schedules and teacher programs will see the danger. Because the machine can take only a certain kind of data, and because the programming becomes more expensive as the number of factors is increased, there is a temptation to tailor the data; that is, the faculty to the machine. Further, since changes are expensive and time-consuming, there is also great hesitancy about remodeling the straitjacket once it has been cut to size. For example, sensible scheduling should consider the health of the professor, his energy pattern, the number of class preparations and even his distance from school. Now, though the machine could consider many of these factors, it cannot do so without increased expense. If an administrator leaves these out of consideration, he may find himself with a very unhappy faculty.

It is for reasons of this sort that the experts insist on the need for greater comprehension of the human element when automation of any sort is installed.[8] It would, after all, be irrational to expect humans to act in accord with the logic of a machine which lacks feelings and real individuality. Unfortunately, the administrator may think otherwise and consider himself freed from the duty of dealing with people.

These few remarks give some idea of why the experts insist that the computers, though they can make some simple decisions between two clear-cut alternatives, cannot exercise that subtle and complex human judgment which is the essence of real management. The automated office may be an aid to management, but it cannot substitute for real managerial responsibility. As a matter of fact, the computers may even increase this responsibility since the need for human relations increases as the demands of routine work decline.[9]

Obligations

Though the evidence and opinions presented will not warrant the presentation of a long catalogue of obligations, they do permit us to affirm the existence of certain broad duties. In the first place, the calculator must always be treated as an aid to and not a substitute for personal decision. A failure on this point may lead to a further weakening of the sense of responsibility even when it does not cause disastrous results.

Since a proper evaluation of the results given by the machines depends on an understanding of its program, goal, limits, and even philosophy, there is a real obligation to study these matters. This is merely to say that the general obligation to be technically competent now includes in its content a duty to understand the new tools available to management.[10] At the same time, it is obvious that the professors of business and of social ethics who are training the future executives should introduce their students to the type of problem we have been studying.

We must, however, be realistic. An understanding of computers is not enough. Unless the executive, his programmers and their consultants have a sound grasp of ethics, and of social ethics in particular, their work may still lead to harmful results. The need to integrate social and ethical factors in decision-making means that there is an obligation to seek for a broader economic theory and the development of new mathematical tools. In the absence of such theory and tools, the temptation to use what is available rather than what is really suitable may cause business to bypass its duties. Admittedly, the formulation of new theories and their translation into formulae which can be handled by the calculator are tremendous tasks. They are also the tasks which must be accomplished if the data processing age is to serve the best interests of business, society and the individual.

All of this merely points to the fact that the real thinking and decision-making is still done by the men involved in the process. It almost tends to indicate that as we are freed from the boredom of routine, it becomes more and more necessary to face the fundamental human problems of a business society. This need not surprise us, for each addition to our effective freedom increases the burden of anxiety and makes us more aware that the conquest of nature still leaves us with the realization of our true destiny and the mastery of ourselves as the ultimate tasks. No machine can liberate us from this obligation; the danger remains, however, that it might cause us to forget it.[11]

NOTES

1. Walter Buckingham, *Automation: Its Impact on Business and People* (New York: Harper and Bros., 1961), p. 50.

2. Norbert Wiener, *Cybernetics* (New York: John Wiley, 1948), pp. 36-37.

3. I have used Norbert Wiener, *The Human Use of Human Beings* (2nd ed., New York: Doubleday, 1954), and G. T. Guilbaud, *What is Cybernetics?* (trans. V. MacKay, New York: Criterion Books, 1959).

4. This is a basic problem in all psychological testing and should not be neglected when the tests are used to work out machine programs.

5. Cited in *Time*, January 11, 1960.

6. Frederick Pollock, *Automation: A Study of its Economic and Social Consequences*, trans. W. O. Henderson and W. H. Chaloner, (New York: Frederick A. Praeger, 1957), p. 224.

7. *Ibid.*, p. 227.

8. Buckingham, *op. cit.*, p. 63, and Pollock, *op. cit.*, p. 223.

9. Pollock, *op. cit.*, p. 219 gives other reasons why automation demands increased executive competence.

10. Buckingham, *op. cit.*, p. 64, and Alexander Henderson and Robert Schlaifer, "Mathematical Programing: Better Information for Better Decision Making," *Harvard Business Review*, 32 (1954), May-June, p. 94.

11. Paul Einzig, *The Economic Consequences of Automation* (New York: W. W. Norton, 1957), p. 246.

CHAPTER 9

AUTOMATION AND THE WELFARE OF THE COUNTRY

by JOSEPH D. KEENAN, *Vice President of AFL-CIO, and International Secretary of the IBEW*

THE ABILITY OF man to make and use tools has given him the ability to change the world. Whether he changes it for the better or for the worse depends not so much on the tools themselves, but on the way he uses them. And the uses to which man puts them depend largely upon his social and moral responsibility. This is what determines his goals.

This holds true for automation, which involves not just new tools, but whole new concepts of the productive process. Automation *will* change the world. It is doing so now. But what the ultimate effect of automation will be on the welfare of our country has not yet been determined. The decision is still ours to make.

A strange thing about this new technology is that so many conflicting statements about it are or could be true. For example: Automation is not new, it is merely the continuation of what has been evolving for years; automation is entirely new and involves new principles never used before. There is truth in both these statements.

Automation will free man from much of the burden of

hard physical work; it will cause more mental strain and increase man's tensions. Both are probably true.

Automation will create new jobs and increase opportunities for employment; it will destroy jobs and cause unemployment. Both true.

Automation will make possible an ever-higher standard of living; it will cause more economic strain and conflict than we have ever experienced before. Again, both are true.

Technological progress began the day the early caveman first picked up a jagged piece of rock and used it as a weapon, or as a tool. It is the alarming rate of incline of today's technology which makes it different from anything in the past. It is the amazing speed with which our new science is being applied to industry which poses the threat to America's workers and to our country.

Water falling from the sky may be a gentle rain or a violent cloudburst. Moving air may be a gentle breeze or a slashing hurricane. Today's technological development has reached cloudburst and hurricane proportions, and we had better quickly get about the business of shoring up our defenses.

It has been said that technology has advanced further in the period since World War II than in the entire previous history of man; that our knowledge is increasing faster today by the hour than it did in earlier times by the century. This is the essential problem. It has far-reaching consequences which challenge many of the traditional aspects of our way of life. Far-reaching changes are needed to bring our social level up to our technological level.

But here we run into the unwillingness and often the outright refusal of many people to accept change—even change which is forced upon us by the physical conditions resulting from modern technology. This is a matter of major concern to organized labor. We want to know where the American worker fits into the new industrial picture. We saw what was happening to many people. We saw jobs disappearing and we began to call attention to what was happening. We prodded industry to recognize the problems and to work with us in meeting them. We were accused of spreading gloom and doom. We were told this was the same old nonsense we had been preaching for years.

For the most part, American industry took the position that there was nothing to worry about, that automation could bring nothing but good. In 1954 a vice-president of one of our largest corporations had this to say:

"The gloom merchants with their cries and laments concerning technological unemployment have always been false prophets. Automation is raising cries of alarm again in these same quarters—and, as always, they will be found to be without foundation." And this corporation official added, "I am certain that any technological advance such as automation can be absorbed in our total economy without even a trace of a ripple on the surface."

Labor did not agree with him then; we certainly do not agree now. Careful study and careful planning are needed. Automation is not the private concern of industry. It has raised problems which demand the best efforts of all of us—labor, management, government and the public. We are encouraged by the fact that more and more people are recognizing this. We are heartened by recent actions of the government in setting up machinery to study these problems. We are pleased at the growing number of conferences, such as this seminar, where these problems are discussed.

As I suggested earlier, the immediate concern of organized labor is what happens to the workers who are caught up in this new industrial revolution. But we have no mind to meet automation in the manner of the French weavers who threw their wooden shoes into the Jacquard looms one hundred and fifty years ago, or of the Luddites of England who believed that the steam age meant the end of the working man and went about the countryside tearing up machinery.

Our intention is not to turn back automation, nor simply to stand in fear of it. Our desire is to meet and accept this new thing, and to help guide it in the direction it must go for human betterment. If we do not, we will find ourselves victimized rather than blessed.

The test, as always, is not how quickly and how cheaply we can produce things; the test is in the effect on the way people live, their economic security, their ability to provide a good education for their children. The machinery of production must be used to serve mankind. It is valuable only to the extent that it helps make possible a happier life and a more wholesome community. This is true for the short run as well as the long run.

Labor agrees with most of what is said about the *potential* benefits of automation. It *can* relieve much of the burden of human drudgery; it *can* make possible levels of production almost undreamed of; it *can* mean a higher standard of living for each and every one of us. Given proper direction, automation can, in the long run, mean all of this and more.

But the transition from old to new can be extremely painful. A prime concern of the labor movement is to make life a little better in the short run. We are concerned about the worker who feels the immediate impact of automation; assurances that in the long run things will be wonderful are of no help to him.

What we say to management is simply this: "We agree with you about the benefits that can come from automation. We welcome it. But when you smash up the old machinery, remember you cannot put the sledge hammer to your workers. Your old equipment is obsolete, but your workers are not. They have served you well; they must not, by themselves, bear the costs of this progress."

We remind management, too, that the new machines can do just about everything but buy the things they make. The more advanced the technology, the greater is the need for increased consumption. Mass production requires mass consumption, and mass consumption can exist only when people have the jobs and the spendable income that permits them to buy. The growing imbalance between our ability to produce and our ability to buy what is produced is the root of many of our current economic troubles.

I do not intend to burden you by repeating statistics on how many millions of Americans today are looking for a job and can't find one. I know you are aware of the dangerously high rate of unemployment, and I'm sure you are familiar with the fact that after each of our past recessions, unemployment has remained at higher and higher levels.

But I would like to take a moment to go behind the overall statistics and bring you just a few indications of what is happening in my own industry. Let me say, first, that the electrical industry is one of the fortunate ones. Automation rests on an electrical and electronic framework.

It has broadened the scope of our work; it has increased the need for craft skills in building, installing, maintaining and servicing of new, specialized equipment. But at the same time, many thousands of our members have been hit directly by loss of jobs, downgrading, transfer out of the bargaining unit, and so forth. Technological change, including automation, was a major factor.

Not long ago we received a letter from the business manager of one of our local unions. His members operated the big electrically controlled overhead cranes in a steel plant. He told us the company was switching to remote, push-button control of the cranes, and that it would mean the elimination of forty jobs. And he asked, "What can we do in a situation like this?"

Recently, in one telephone system organized by the IBEW, there were over two thousand fewer employees on the payroll at the end of the year than at the beginning. Some of those retained were down-graded to lower-paying jobs. At the same time, the company's profits for the year hit an all-time high and the average number of daily calls reached a new record.

In radio and television broadcasting, remote operation of transmitters along with automatic program switchers and other new equipment have eliminated thousands of jobs and job opportunities.

A manufacturing plant in Scranton, Pennsylvania, which once employed four hundred IBEW members, has completely stopped all production activities. The work was transferred to an automated plant in another state where it could be done more cheaply, with fewer employees. This plant closing left four hundred of our members jobless in an area which has long been classified as a distressed area, where jobs are virtually impossible to find.

A small manufacturing plant in Connecticut, which employed eighty of our members for a good many years, installed two new machines, operated by two employees, and left twenty-five of our members without work.

Our electric utility companies, faced with greater and greater demands for power, are themselves speeding the trend to automation. We saw the world's largest gas turbine generating plant, producing one hundred thousand kw, go into operation without a living soul within fifteen miles of it. The plant is controlled remotely.

A Chicago utility has installed an automatic dispatch

system which uses computers to regulate production in ten separate plants handling more than ninety per cent of the company's total capacity. A Pennsylvania utility formerly employed ninety-three men in the operations and test division. After automation the number dropped to forty— a loss of fifty-three jobs in this one department. Employment at a New England electric company is down forty per cent in ten years due to the automation of distribution sub-stations and the installation of new work practices. In the railroad industry, a recent survey revealed that in the last two years we have lost more than twelve hundred jobs for electricians, helpers, and apprentices.

I could cite many examples from the electrical industry and from others where the impact has been much more severe. Men with fifteen, twenty and even more years seniority have been affected. And the predictions of things to come portend an even greater impact in the years ahead.

Radical changes in technology always create some dislocations. Old work skills are made obsolete and new skills are required. Some types of work are eliminated; entire industries or parts of industries are wiped out and new ones are created. There are changes in industry location which affect entire communities and regions.

Organized labor realizes that automation provides the basis for great benefits. The present advanced stage of technology in the United States is testimony to the acceptance of technological advances by the American people, and to the cooperative efforts of organized labor.

In my own union, the IBEW, many of our contracts contain a clause which states: "The parties to this agreement recognize that a continuing improvement in the standard of living of employees depends upon technological progress." It states further that this improvement depends upon a cooperative attitude on the part of all parties in achieving such progress.

But organized labor insists that the burdens of rapid change must be cushioned. We say that management and society, who stand to benefit from technological change, must assume their responsibilities in protecting the workers, their families and their communities against the hazards of radical changes. In our sense of values, human beings and human welfare are more important than machines and new methods. In counting the costs of automation we cannot stop with the costs of buildings and machines. We must include also the costs of helping people and their communities adjust to the change. The substitution of machine skill for human skill must not result in reduced living standards for a large number of workers, even over the short run.

Unions have found that much can be done through collective bargaining, through labor-management cooperation, to ease the impact of automation. For example, here are a few of the things that IBEW locals have done.

A recent agreement with a maker of automatic broadcast equipment set up a retraining program for radio station employees displaced by use of the company's equipment and program services. This IBEW agreement is the first of its kind in the broadcast industry, which has been hard hit by automation. It calls for payment of tuition and fees at established schools, so that displaced radio station personnel will have the opportunity to learn new skills, either in the broadcast industry or in other fields.

Another agreement provides that any new automatic machines that require an operator will be manned by a member of the union. If necessary, he will be retrained by the employer or the company supplying the machine.

Other agreements guarantee that workers with a certain amount of service, say three or five years, will not be laid off or have their pay reduced during the term of the contract because of lack of work.

Many locals have negotiated clauses calling for advance notification and joint consultation when major changes are planned. The decision to automate is usually not made quickly, and equipment is ordered long before its installation.

During this time, careful planning and thoughtful action by both the union and management can contribute toward an orderly adjustment to the change. One such clause negotiated by the IBEW states: "The company agrees that when a decision is reached by management to install automatic equipment, the brotherhood will be informed. Any changes that affect the members of the brotherhood shall be negotiated."

Union efforts at the bargaining table are aimed not only at reducing the hardships that can accompany the introduction of automation, but also at trying to insure that the workers on the job share in the benefits of increased productivity. This means that our negotiations involve such things as the content, classification and wage rates of new or changed jobs, the selection of workers to fill these jobs, and wage and fringe increases based upon increased productivity. We have to negotiate on these things because we know they do not come automatically.

Among the seven "Management Principles of Automation" approved by a majority of corporation officials who took part in one magazine poll was this one: "The company is entitled to *all* of the savings from mechanization." Another one stated: "We are not obligated to compensate mechanization-displaced workers."

Fortunately, not all employers have this callous attitude. Many IBEW locals have negotiated agreements providing a cushion for the worker whose job is eliminated. They include provisions for retraining, as I mentioned earlier, and for giving the displaced worker a chance to qualify for other jobs with the company. They include transfer rights, with seniority protection, to other locations of the company. In some cases, part or all of the worker's relocation costs are paid.

Other cushioning measures include:

Severance pay, providing lump sum payments to workers when it is impossible to avoid layoffs.

Supplemental unemployment benefits, which provide additional weekly payments to the worker while he looks for a new job.

Provisions for early retirement.

Extension of welfare benefits such as life insurance and medical care plans for a specified period, or until the worker finds a new job.

Unions have, altogether, developed a wide variety of procedures, not to oppose or restrict automation, but to provide concrete aid for workers and their families who feel its impact. From our experience in this area we have learned two things. First, collective bargaining can and should play an important role in meeting some of the problems in the work place arising from automation. Certainly, the bargaining table is the proper place to meet the problems relating directly to the job.

The second thing we have learned is that collective bargaining, by itself, is not enough. The problems of automation are of such a scope that they cannot be met fully on an individual plant basis, or even on an industry basis. In many cases, the relief provided through collective bargaining is only temporary. It is designed to tide the worker over until he can find another job. But what happens when no other jobs are available?

The same holds true for retraining. Certainly, retraining is necessary, and it is valuable, but only to the extent that it qualifies displaced workers for other available jobs. There is no value in training men for jobs that do not exist. These plans cannot create jobs in areas where unemployment is rising. The fact is that nothing which can be done at the bargaining table, nothing which can be done by joint labor-management committees, will have real meaning unless our economy is healthy enough and growing fast enough to provide jobs for everyone who wants and needs them.

We have heard the theories which say that automation will create more jobs than it destroys, that new industries will arise to replace the old, that big boosts in white-collar and service trades employment will more than compensate for the drop in blue-collar jobs. So far, we have not seen any signs that this is true, at least not for the immediate future. Instead, as automation is more fully developed and as it spreads into new areas, the problems are intensified by further reductions in job opportunities.

Automation already has made tremendous headway in banks, insurance companies, and other offices throughout the country. A study in San Francisco showed that for every five office workers eliminated by electronic data processing, only one job was created. Congressman Holland of the House Labor Committee, in a preliminary report to the President earlier this year, noted that machines could eliminate some four million office and clerical jobs in the next five years. Certainly this would leave no room for taking up the slack in blue-collar employment.

Automation also is moving into the service trades. In the retail sales industry, which is the nation's largest service industry, automatic equipment is being used in accounting and merchandise control operations, in the warehousing and handling of goods, and even in automatic vending on the selling floor of our food and department stores. Engineers believe the completely automated supermarket can be a reality within the very near future.

Where do we take up the employment slack here? Some employers have been frank enough to admit that the main attraction of automatic equipment is that it can cut down the expense and problems associated with live workers.

If technological changes are introduced gradually in an economy where production and employment are increasing rapidly enough, social and economic dislocations can be minimized. There would still be problems, of course, but in a rapidly growing economy they would be manageable. Procedures developed through collective bargaining, retraining programs, and improved social legislation would be more effective.

However, this has not been the case. Technical change has been radical, it has been widespread, and it has been rapid. Moreover, it has been accompanied by a slowdown of economic growth. Production, sales, and jobs have not increased enough to provide employment for a growing labor force and for displaced workers. Thus, many of the potential social benefits of automation have been wasted. Much of the economy's rising productivity and growing labor force have not been translated into expanded production of needed goods and services, but rather into rising unemployment and part-time work, idle plants and machines, and a growing number of distressed communities.

We don't know yet what the increase in productivity, or output per manhour, will be this year. But an increase of only 2½ per cent would mean a labor displacement of 1,500,000 workers. If the productivity increase is 3 per cent, displacement would be nearly 2,000,000 workers.

If total real production increases as much as productivity, these workers would be reabsorbed. But such a slow rate of growth is not sufficient. A much higher rate is needed to provide jobs for the existing number of unemployed, and for new workers just entering the labor market.

Many specific and localized problems relating to automation can be handled through collective bargaining, labor-management cooperation, and joint community efforts. But a more rapid rate of economic growth is the basic necessity for realizing the full benefits of automation. And the major responsibility for achieving this rests with the federal government, through its spending, tax, and budget policies.

America needs the greatly increased production that automation makes possible. We need it to improve the living conditions of millions of American families, to provide adequate public services, to strengthen our national defense, to provide assistance for the peoples of under-developed and newly emerging nations, and to help them along the road to independence and freedom.

But the mere existence of automatic machines does not mean that they will be used fully and wisely, or that the benefits they make possible will be shared by all. Problems must be met, decisions made, and policies adopted by men, not machines. And we must have modern policies to match our modern equipment.

Easing the burdens of technological change and achieving a fair and widespread distribution of its benefits is a goal to which American labor is dedicated. Throughout its history labor has been dedicated to the cause of social and economic justice. In many respects its goals parallel the teachings of the Catholic Church, and it has received the official sanction and encouragement of the Church.

American trade unions are, in fact, one of the greatest forces in carrying out the principles laid down in the great social encyclicals of Pope Leo XIII seventy years ago, of Pope Pius XI forty years later, and now of Pope John XXIII, who has pointed out the benefits offered by our new technology and the responsibilities that go with it.

American labor has been a tremendous force for good in our society. It has been the driving force in achieving many of the things we all cherish today. Not enough people realize this. Too many people have been confused and misled by distorted and overpublicized charges against a tiny fraction of the labor movement. They have been swept up in an atmosphere of distrust, suspicion, and downright antagonism toward *all* unions.

The record needs to be set straight. We are grateful for what the Church has done and is doing to explain and interpret the true nature of the labor movement. We are grateful for the criticisms and suggestions offered by the Church as a friend. We look to you for continued support and guidance.

American labor has tried, to the best of its ability, to live up to its social and moral responsibilities. We earnestly want to continue to do so. This is the job of all of us—labor, management, government, the Church, and the public: to understand our responsibilities as they apply to each of us, to accept them, and to work together in fulfilling them. How well we do this will determine to what extent our tools, with which we can change the world, will be used for the benefit of all mankind.

CHAPTER 10

MANY FACETS
OF THE PROBLEM

by JOHN O'NEIL, *Chairman, Finance Committee*
General Tire and Rubber Company

I THINK IT WAS three or four months ago that the seminar director extended a kind invitation to me to address this group. Since that time I have been jotting down some random notes and comments bearing on the general subject of automation.

Last week when I began to reshuffle my notes and get them lined up for my talk today, I found that I had not one but three different speeches. Rather I should say that I had speeches on three different subjects. And I think it is an interesting commentary on the whole problem that all three subjects continued to crop up in my mind as I was preparing for this seminar.

Naturally I found I had dozens of notes on the economic and social aspects of automation itself. And, of course, that will be my principal subject today.

But I also kept running across notes here and there on a second, somewhat different subject which, for want of a better title, could be called "Our Basic Form of Government": the pros and cons of democracy, of our representative form of government as it is practiced today. Frankly, I found I had enough material on that subject alone to fill a book.

And the third subject which continued to crop up in my notes was also one to which a person could devote an entire course. For want of a better title, I think this subject might properly be called "The Temporal and the Eternal." In other words, I found myself continually intrigued with and grappling with the very basic problem of the relationship between this world and the next.

I think it is quite significant that these three major problems kept cropping up in my mind at the same time. And although in this discussion I plan to concentrate on automation, if now and then the other two subjects show a tendency to intrude, I hope you won't blame it entirely on the fact that I did not do a very good job of reshuffling my notes.

With that preliminary, let's proceed to the problem.

Even a definition of automation is rather hard to come by. I have a friend who says automation is just a Madison Avenue word for mechanization. He would say that the invention of the wheel marked the beginning of automation. Our chief economist sees the new element in automation as the introduction of control systems to run the machines. I suppose it's a matter of degree.

For my purpose here, I'm thinking of automation as a machine, or rather a complex series of machines, coupled with techniques and processes, capable of doing a rather complicated series of operations which would normally require the efforts of many men.

For the purpose of my definition, I am prescinding from the point of whether in fact the automation machinery actually does displace workers or not. Very often the introduction of a large electronic computer into a company does not necessarily mean the actual displacement of working personnel; it may merely mean that with the addition of the machine the company is now able to do many things it never could have done before.

Actually, regardless of your definition, the problem of automation is not a new problem at all but simply an old problem under a new name.

Some will see it as a threat to their jobs and therefore something to be opposed. Others will see it as one more step on what they call science's road to a perfect world. Others will see it as a new weapon in their hands to beat the unions. Still others will see it as a new item which they can sell and thereby profit from. Unfortunately, in the world in which we live human beings tend to see any problem or concept solely from their own viewpoint. Sometimes they do this consciously and deliberately; sometimes unconsciously.

Hence there arises what we may call for want of a better term the "adversary system." This adversary system seems to be almost the rule of conduct under which most, if not all, elements of our society work. Like the prosecuting attorney in a lawsuit, you emphasize your own point of view, stress your own assets and presume that the other party in the debate will stress his own assets. Often you exaggerate; certainly you select. And you justify this exaggeration and selection by estimating that your opponent will make the same exaggerations in his own behalf. If the invention of the adversary system can be laid at the door of any one man, and I am sure that it cannot, that man would probably argue that, in his opinion and in the present state of human nature, the adversary system is the best means, fallible though it certainly is, of producing true justice. And perhaps it does produce justice in many cases. But at any one point in time, and listening to the arguments of any one citizen who is "naturally" defending, emphasizing, exaggerating his own viewpoint, the picture is quite a mixed one.

Thus in the so-called problem of automation, the adversary system makes its presence known, even though its actual proponents may be completely unaware of the existence and influence of this system on their own lives and arguments.

There is a rather famous story which I think illustrates the problem of automation better than anything else I know. A company had been hired to dig a trench for laying some sewer lines and they had a very complex ditch-digging machine at work. One of the bystanders who happended to be very interested in seeing the machine work watched for a few minutes, then walked up to the foreman and said, "You know, I think you ought to get rid of that machine and you could put a hundred men to work with picks and shovels." The foreman said, "Well, if you put it that way, I wonder why we would not put a thousand men to work with teaspoons."

Actually the problem of automation is not quite so simple as the ditch-digging story makes it appear. It's a pretty tough subject and has many aspects.

And when you are listening to anyone talk on the subject of automation, remember he may be talking about only one or two or three of a dozen or more possible aspects of the problem. And so you must appraise his opinion in light of his viewpoint.

It is my purpose today to point out not one but many aspects, many facets, many viewpoints of the problem with the object of working toward an overall integral approach.

First, I plan to discuss three "sets" of aspects under which the problem may be viewed. Then I would like to propose three basic principles which are fundamental to any solution of the problem and, above all, a fourth, overriding principle which controls and governs the other three and which I have called the "super-principle."

And so, the first set of aspects under which the problem can be viewed: for want of better terminology, let us call one side the material or segmented aspect and the other the integral approach. They are really different aspects, separate and distinct, at least in principle, and yet so interwoven that there will be continual overlapping in any person's discussion of the two aspects, no matter how he may try to keep them separated. It is something like trying to keep man's body and soul separate in appraising his actions.

I am afraid that too many of our great brains in the world today view the problem from only the first aspect. They consider automation as purely an economic problem, purely a scientific phenomenon.

But since the prime figure in automation or any other economic problem is not a simple machine, but man, a child of God, brother of Christ, and destined by God for an eternal share in His own life, it is man and his character, destiny, and dignity which are the controlling factors in this problem.

Even if you are aware of this, however, you can still be hopelessly confused. A priest would not be very competent in giving a moral opinion on a medical subject if he knew absolutely nothing about the medical facts involved. By the same token, to form any sound opinion on the problem of automation, it is essential that the judge scrutinize very thoroughly the material aspect of the problem: that is, the basic economic facts involved.

If he did not, he might be very inclined to pass judgment almost immediately when a new machine threw the father of a family out of his job and brought social distress and hardship to the family. It is not nearly so simple as that.

Before you can truly understand the whole, you must understand the parts. It is essential, therefore, for a student of this problem to be very soundly aware of the economic aspects of automation.

The popes have given outstanding examples of the inte-

131

gral, overall approach. Pius XII in particular had a remarkable interest in the technical aspects of the occupations of the people in his audiences. During the course of
his pontificate, he must have addressed several hundred different professional and occupational groups and nearly
always talked to them about the technical side of their
occupation—as well as its spiritual aspects.

I recall several years ago receiving a very graphic illustration of this. The head of one of our plastics companies
had just returned from a trip to Rome and told us with
great astonishment of an audience he attended in the
Vatican in which the pope had talked about the prospects
for polyethylene—and this at a time when our own research scientists were just becoming familiar with this new
synthetic.

And Dr. Paul Dudley White, Eisenhower's heart physi-
cian, after hearing Pius XII address a congress of doctors
on the subject of cardiology, made the remark that the
talk was the best discussion he had ever heard on the subject of heart disease.

The next set of aspects under which the problem could
be viewed I have called the "micro" and "macro." For example, a person could consider the problem of automation
primarily from the viewpoint of the individual, and see
how it benefits him, how it creates advantages or disadvantages for him as an individual. He could also consider
it from the viewpoint of how it benefits or hurts various
groups of which the individual is a member, such as the
company or industry in which the man works, the country
or nation in which he resides, the world in which he is a
pilgrim here on earth.

Let's take a microscopic view of these different sectors
into which the problem can be segregated. And for the
sake of procedure and convenience, let's consider the individual in both his roles somewhat simultaneously. After
all, as a worker in a company, as a citizen of a country,

and as a resident of the world, some of the benefits and disadvantages which accrue to the particular group considered will also obviously accrue to him as a member of that group. In addition, of course, he does have specific aspects of his own and we will consider them also. It is like the old problem of public and private good.

First, then, the company and its employees, stockholders, and customers. Remember one thing—a worker's job is safest when he works for a company which is successful and which makes a profit. It would seem to me that the following advantages accrue to a company which had made a successful application of automation:

a) greater survival potential;

b) greater capacity to share wages and dividend increases and price reductions;

c) generally speaking, better morale and job security (for morale is better and jobs are safer in an efficient and profit-making organization; in fact, needless tasks, wastage, featherbedding, and inefficiencies destroy morale, decrease job security, and even attack man's very dignity).

Fifty years ago there were over one hundred tire companies in existence; today there are about ten. There were many causes for their failure, but I will say this for sure: that the ones which did not mechanize, modernize, automate, and keep up with the times are out of business today. Where are the jobs of their employees now?

I think it might be opportune at this time to have a little digression on the meaning of profit. This is a word which should be very clearly understood by everyone, but particularly by someone discussing the problem of automation. And yet I am afraid that there are very few people who understand it.

Perhaps I can illustrate the problem by an example

from our own company: In the last ten years, our company earned, before taxes, some fifteen to fifty million dollars per year. This amounts to over two hundred million dollars in profits since 1950. We have paid out a relatively small amount in dividends, actually less than 2 per cent on the present stock market price a person would pay for a share of our stock.

And yet we have had to borrow approximately one hundred million dollars just to stay in business. This is because profit does not mean cash, does not mean dividends. Our so-called profit has had to be reinvested in additional tires, additional inventory of various kinds, additional machinery and equipment, additional buildings.

But the government figures that we have made a big profit and has charged us over a hundred million dollars in corporate income taxes. I might better have said that we had to borrow one hundred million dollars in order to pay our taxes.

Meanwhile, by the way, we have grown from nearly ten thousand employees to over forty thousand.

Of course, there are disadvantages in a company which automates. Layoffs are by no means pleasant for anyone involved. In fairness to automation, however, I think it should be pointed out that automation is not always the "bogey-man." Sometimes it is a simple case of efficiencies in management which have nothing to do with machines.

And remember, above all, the worst layoffs of all come about in the unsuccessful company which did not keep up with the times.

Thus, looking at it from the standpoint of the company as such, the answer is pretty obvious.

Like a company, a country is "competing" in the world. If it can produce better products at a lower cost, this will mean not only a higher standard of living at home but will also mean that the country can sell its products abroad. For some countries (England for example), these two factors are almost synonymous. To be in this position, however, it must have a sound economic structure. It cannot encourage or foster inefficiencies or waste. Even as it is desirable for an individual *company* within a country to modernize and to become more efficient, so *vis-à-vis* the other countries in the world, it is very desirable for a *country* to become an efficient producer.

And if by automating the country as a whole is able to turn out the same goods and services with 20 per cent fewer people, it would seem fairly obvious that it is in a much stronger economic position than it was when it was turning out the same goods and services with 100 per cent of its labor force. Now it has 20 per cent additional men to employ in other worthwhile services and can actually increase its total output.

Just as "profit" for a company must be clearly understood, so also must "cost" to a country. Sometimes what we term "cost" is not cost at all as far as the country is concerned but simply a transfer or redistribution of funds. For example, President Kennedy has been talking of spending fifty billion dollars to send a man to the moon. He has also been discussing an additional three and two-tenths billion for additional expenses this year. Both these figures require a little bit of understanding. If it were one company or one individual disbursing this amount of money, this could truly be called a cost or expenditure as far as that company or individual is concerned. However, it must be remembered that when you are talking about cost to a country as a whole, very often what is paid out of one pocket simply goes into another pocket—not out of the country. Sometimes it is easier to understand a complex problem when you look at it from the standpoint of a small group, like the family. Suppose you were to pay your brother ten dollars to mow the lawn. You would be out-of-pocket by ten dollars, but if you view the two of you as one family, the family has not spent ten dollars.

Looking at cost from the viewpoint of the country as a whole (and excluding payments to other nations), it seems to me that the only true cost is the usage or consumption of human or material resources. In other words, the fifty billion dollars that Mr. Kennedy is talking about will be paid, for the most part, to American workers, directly or indirectly. We will use x million man-hours in the moon-shot effort and will expend a certain amount of natural material resources; but if both happen to be "surplus" or available at the time, it may well be that we have had no cost at all.

And, if by automation we are able to turn out in 1962 all the material goods and services which we turned out in 1961 and do this with 10 or 25 or 40 per cent fewer people, doesn't it mean that these displaced persons are in a sense "surplus" and available for employment on the moonshot?

Actually, I have oversimplified the problem for example purposes. The people freed by automation are not likely to be the ones or certainly not *all* the ones we will need for the moonshot.

But they would be free for other worthwhile projects. And you don't have to look very far in this country of ours to see that there are millions of things just crying to be done. Our road systems are badly in need of substantial improvement. We need hospital beds. I have seen an estimate by the Public Health Service indicating that for the 1960 population we needed something over 2,000,000 hospital beds for civilians alone. Actually we had 1,175,000 beds, making a shortage of almost 900,000. There are hundreds of other examples in the field of education, medicine, and housing.

Doesn't it make sense to say that if we can turn out the

automobiles, the homes, the tires, the airplanes, the refrigerators, the stoves, and all the other goods and services we are able to turn out, and if we can turn them out with fewer people, we then make these people available for employment on other worthwhile projects?

Of course, the transfer or reemployment of our work force is not simple, particularly in America. Because in America we try to solve our problems without sacrificing our personal freedom, and sometimes we abuse this right. Because of the free society in which we live and the various forms of substitute compensations which have grown up during the years, the mobility of our work force is far less than in some other countries.

We Americans have to a great degree led a sheltered life. Frankly, we are remarkably ignorant of the facts of international trade as well as politics.

Several years ago, I took a trip to our factory in Venezuela. En route, our ship stopped at a little island in the Caribbean named Curaçao. We were there three or four hours and I rented a car and rode around the island. The taxi driver was really amazing. Frankly, he knew more about international finance than I did. He was very much aware of what his country produced, what it sold, what countries it traded with, what their balance of trade was, what their total exports and imports were each year. He knew that his country had to be competitive in the world markets in order for them to eat and live. He was very much aware of true cost and its elements. Too few Americans are.

Similarly, too few of our people, from the top on down, understand the real difference between redistributing wealth and producing it. A greater and greater percentage of our people are devoting themselves to ways and plans of "cutting the pie" into different shares, and fewer and fewer are working to produce more pies.

If automation does nothing else, it may force Americans

137

to face the economic facts of life. It could be a great opportunity.

It certainly seems to me to be an incredible paradox when there is so much national worry about joblessness from automation and yet so much work to be done.

Looking at the problem from the standpoint of the world: Many of the things said elsewhere apply here. Incredible advantages are possible from automation in underdeveloped countries; and, as far as joblessness on a worldwide scale is concerned, this also should be a needless worry. There is plenty of work to be done worldwide. The world should seek ways to do it more quickly, efficiently, and thus free people for the next job.

Another set of aspects which I will mention only in passing could be called the abstract and the concrete, the theoretical and the practical, the ideal and the real, the goal and the here and now. The differences here could fill a book but time is running short and I would like to outline for you certain principles which I think are basic in any solution of this problem we are discussing.

Whenever I look at the problem of automation or any similar problems in the field of economics, it seems to me that there are three basic principles which govern:

(1) We should not perpetuate or even encourage waste and inefficiency. They may be tolerated for brief periods of time in the interest of a higher good. But generally speaking, if a new or efficient, more economical method of doing anything is developed, it should be fostered.

(2) At the same time, we must face the fact that these new, more efficient methods may cause disruption to our present state of being, and some provision must be made to alleviate the problems caused by this disruption.

(3) The means we choose to alleviate the troubles caused by the disruption must not be so palliative that they will dull or drug the recipients into a state of passive acceptance from which they have no ambition to extricate themselves. Generally speaking, the means should be temporary, like medicine, to cover the trials of the transition period. In isolated cases, they might be lifelong, like medicine taken by the incurable diabetic; but these should be isolated cases, not the general rule.

Overriding even these principles, however, is the very basic principle (which I have called the "super-principle") that man must use the goods of this world in a way which is in keeping with his natural and supernatural dignity. If a particular usage of the goods of this world hinders rather than helps man toward his natural perfection and final supernatural goal, then there is something wrong with that particular usage. In short, the Christian concept is far different from the communistic idea of economics. We regard material things as means, as helps, not as the final end.

Of course it is very difficult to live by or accomplish the three basic principles which I enumerated above. They seem so obvious, so correct. And yet, partly because of the adversary system and partly because of the great anonymity behind which all the major forces at work in our society operate, one or more of the principles will be completely neglected.

Thus, for example, the industrialist will subscribe wholeheartedly to the first principle; namely, that there should be no waste, no inefficiency, and that economic, efficient methods should be fostered and encouraged. He may even agree in theory that the disruption caused by the new efficient methods should be alleviated. But he may very probably say, "That is someone else's problem; I've got my hands full with my own." Or he may try to do something on his own and find that the problem is too big for him. One company in an industry is usually limited to some degree. Perhaps even one industry in a country is similarly limited. Or he may want to help and actually try to help and find that the union with whom he is dealing, once they are given an inch, will take the mile. In these days of the adversary system, coupled with collective bargaining, each side is reluctant to offer the other side anything. Frankly, there are dozens of companies who probably would have given their employees many benefits except that they did not want to be forced to negotiate these benefits with the union leaders.

The working man and the labor union will of course subscribe to my second principle; namely, that the disruption caused by new methods must be provided for. However, they will be very reluctant to accept the first or the third principle. They will object to the first principle because they will say, and rightly so, that adequate provision has not as yet been made for the disruption caused by the new methods. They will object to the third principle: namely, that the remedy provided for the disruption should be temporary or isolated, rather than permanent and universal. They will want to be as well off when disrupted as they were when working full time. Hence a kind of stalemate.

There is one more force at work in our society which makes the problem even more difficult. This is a force which, for want of a better name, I call extreme democracy. Maybe we should call it enforced mediocrity—or the great levelling-off process, or extreme nondiscrimination. I don't mean nondiscrimination in the color sense or in the race sense. I don't approve of that type of discrimination at all. I am not talking about that here; nor am I

140

talking about true democracy, but rather extreme democracy, which plays its role in the pseudo principle that "We must treat everybody equally." Someone once said that there is nothing more inequitable than the equal treatment of unequals. And yet this principle, coupled with the great propensity we have for putting everything down into a law and spelling out the great details (often because we don't trust the local administrator to have any intelligence, honesty, or prudence) makes the realization of my three principles almost impossible. The legislator says if we are going to give it to one, we have to give it to all; the working man says if you are going to pay him three dollars an hour, then you have to pay me three dollars an hour, too; the politician says if we are going to give this special benefit to this group of people, then we have to find a special benefit to give to another group of people too. So, as a consequence, we do nothing.

So what do we do? In the spiritual life it is said, "First sanctify yourself, then you will be able to sanctify others." The same thing applies here. Before you can help others reach a solution, you must understand the true problems yourself and the basic principles which apply. You must put the problem in its proper perspective. It is a problem not only now but a problem of the future. You must beware of solutions which keep people from working. True wealth is only produced by human labor.

As I see it, the overall aspect demands a positive vote for automation, but solutions must be found for the problems it may cause. In appraising various applications of automation and various solutions to the problems it may cause, beware of "emotions of the moment." Consider all aspects. View them in light of the integral, overall approach, the "Big Three" basic principles, and above all, the Super-Principle.

Work toward a better understanding of the true mean-

141

ing of "cost," and "profit," and "wealth" and its production and distribution. Don't encourage inefficiency and waste.

Work continually for the solution of problems efficiency sometimes produces. But don't make the cure worse than the disease. If necessary, accept the "temporary" solution, but only temporarily, and recognize it as a detour, not the road.

Remember that the economy is for men, not men for the economy, but don't misapply this principle. In short, be realistic idealists.

CHAPTER 11

THE PROMOTION OF
ETHICS BY AUTOMATION

by GEORGE M. MUSCHAMP, *Vice President,*
Engineering, Industrial Products Group,
Minneapolis-Honeywell Regulator Co.

IN ITS MAJOR ASPECTS, the ethical evaluation of automation cannot be separated from the general economic fabric of which it is only a part. There are some unique characteristics of automation to be indicated. Mainly, however, automation is bound up with the processes for producing goods if, as assumed, we are limiting our discussion to the automation of commerce and industry and not including automation of the home or of recreation, which have their own significant sets of ethical effects. We should, therefore, look at the more generic effect which is that resulting from technological change.

It is easy to grow cynical about the ethical effects of technological change because some of the transient effects rightly or wrongly attributed to it appear unhealthy in the extreme. Not all writers have been able to resist this temptation and their theses sometimes do not reflect credit upon themselves nor upon those who accept their pessimism.

The Prophets of Doom

We have seen treatment, in a whole batch of books purporting to be serious, of such characters as the executive, the organization man, the status seeker, the operator, and the waste maker, and such places as the brave new world. The last mentioned has even been revisited. Collectively, these books picture a society populated by men who are unethical, devoid of individuality and having a very bleak ethical future as a result of technological change.

In part, this body of literature exposes some very seamy aspects of our society. We should all welcome this exposure to the end that we get at the causes and correct them rather than sweep them under the rug. Nor do I object to the humorous treatments as pure fun, down to but not including the sick comedians. What I do object to are the statements and implications in prediction of a dour long-range result of technological change.

Technology Combats the Population Problem

In my view, technological change is the one hope of combatting the complex situation that we now face, resulting from biological not technological causes. Isn't it perfectly obvious that even the large technological attainments we have made in the past have fallen far short of supplying the world population with the minimal requirements of what we consider a decent living? We must do much more to come even close to meeting the demands of the explosive population growth. A more even distribution of the existing wealth would not result in any substantial improvement in the average condition.

144

Positively Plan the Ethical as Well as Material Future

If we accept the idea that great technological change is essential to meeting the needs of large masses of people, we can then concentrate upon a constructive approach to accomplish it instead of wasting our time in dwelling upon the question of whether it is actually good for us and why it might not be. Make a positive rather than a negative approach, an approach which recognizes bad things as problems that have to be overcome, not reasons for abandoning hope of success for the project. This is one project we cannot abandon and we should stop picturing it as a material success and an ethical failure. Let us picture it as both a material *and* an ethical success.

People, not Machines, Have Ethics

In assessing the ethical effect of technological change and automation specifically, sight is sometimes lost of the very obvious fact that machines do not have ethics, a characteristic possessed only by the people who use machines. The ethical effect, therefore, is concerned with the morals of people who use technological instruments of all kinds, use them in the broadest sense of the word, which includes particularly those managers who provide machines for the use of others.

The straight razor used in its intended way is ethically acceptable. Not so when it is used for slitting throats. The electrical razor was an ethical as well as a technological advance because, as a blunt instrument, its unethical use is somewhat limited. Unfortunately, many of our instruments of automation do not contain safeguards against unethical use. But no amount of complexity can obscure the fact that the ethical or unethical use depends utterly

145

upon the user—the person. When we consider the good and bad of automation, therefore, we are considering the good and bad of people.

To compare the morals of people today against some earlier time is beyond the scope of this discussion. It is extremely important but not really in point in this discussion of automation to consider whether people are better or worse ethically except as the change has resulted from technological change of automation. There has been some confusion of the effect of automation with the effect of bigness simply because big organizations often find automation necessary for their survival. While the division of responsibility in organizations can conceivably divide ethical responsibility to the vanishing point, this is not attributable to technology or automation but to people again, a large group of people.

The Double Standard of Ethics

It has been emphasized by many, including John C. Bennett in his *Theological Conception of Goals for Economic Life,* that there is widespread use of a double standard of ethics by business people.

An early British patent on a firearm specified that it would shoot round bullets against Christians and square bullets against Turks. Some of us, it is said, are shooting round bullets on Sundays and square bullets on weekdays. I think this is true and is likely to remain true as long as people feel they have to compromise their ethical standards in order to survive. At the national level (as against communism), it would appear that fundamentally we are protecting our moral position, our way of life. While it may be more than incidental that we are also protecting our material position, this is secondary. Our progress toward the single standard of ethics is bound to be a long process even when material gains eliminate some of the motivation for unethical practice. Sound as Emery Reeves' *Anatomy of Peace* appears to many people, it is unrealistic to suppose that people will throw in with supraorganization at any level unless they are convinced that the larger organization will in fact improve their lot even to preserving their existing level of ethics.

Ethical Progress through Automation

Automation, far from impeding this progress, is in my view one of the greatest contributors to it. What reason is there to suppose that such progress does exist? What reason is there for optimism about this allegedly materialistic society?

The basic reason for optimism is that automation replaces lower order functions, freeing people for higher order functions. What these higher order functions are or should be is for the ethical specialists, including the clergy, to decide and promote. Whatever they are, people have increasingly more time in which to examine them and perform them. It is true that in many cases, perhaps in most cases at this stage, this time is devoted to frivolous pursuits, and, from an ethical standpoint, this may be retrogression. This, however, is the challenge to the ethical people and I believe that with their help, people *en masse* will give more attention to ethical improvement. However slowly it may seem to be moving, the brotherhood of man is evolving as evidenced by the favorable change in relation of individual to individual. We have progressed from the serf of medieval times to the not too happy employee of Industrial Revolution times to the present employee who often asserts himself individually and more often collectively.

No one seriously questions any longer the fact that automation calls for higher skills. Even labor leaders today are asking mainly for assurance against workers being displaced. They are seeking education of the workers for better jobs. Ethically, this can be viewed in terms of raising the dignity and spiritual outlook of the individual and the decline of collectivism.

Ethical Responsibility for Automation

There is increasing evidence, too, that ethical responsibility for automation is increasing. It is appropriate that the federal government should take leadership in this field and their efforts in the office automation field are well documented in the reports of the House Subcommittee on Census and Government Statistics. Here two opposed problems are apparent.

One is the possibility of the dislocation of people which has turned out to be far less a problem than the pessimists feared. In any event, the necessary steps of retraining and reassignment have been taken for the protection of the people whose work might be affected.

The other is the problem of insuring that increased production through automation is indeed realized and that increased efficiency is not dissipated in unnecessary work.

Private organizations are similarly recognizing the necessity to plan large automation activities with regard for the effect on the workers.

The Special Ethical Contribution of Automation

It has been indicated that for the most part automation's effects are inseparable from those of technological change generally. One part of automation which is unique is that of control concepts, applicable to many, many aspects of society. This is related, for example, to the endless controversy between the advocates of tight government controls and those who oppose them. Ethical factors of great effect are involved here.

How Much Control?

The idea that the state impose economic and ethical limitations on the development of commerce and industry is established in many areas such as communications, utilities, transportation, food, drugs, clothing, shelter, and safety. The antitrust laws run across all industry and their administration has been continually tightened. Voluntary limitations have also been imposed in some areas without legislation. It should not be said categorically that those who feel unduly bridled by these limitations are unethical because there is genuine question as to whether some of these limitations are in the public interest. The motivation of those who prosecute the limitations has, on occasion, also been questioned.

On the other hand, the utterly free play of the applicable forces cannot be relied upon to effect the proper control ethically or economically as Bennett has also pointed out. Those of us who deal with automation and particularly automatic control understand perfectly that some systems are inherently stable and can safely be permitted a degree of self-regulation while other systems are unstable and without the proper external constraints will destroy themselves. It should be recognized that the addition of the wrong corrective measure to the unstable system will hasten its collapse. Neither too much too soon nor too little too late will do.

We do not know how to identify the characteristics of ethical systems in terms that would enable us specifically to apply this experience. Attempts have been made to ap-

149

ply known control principles to economic systems that include ethical considerations like "propensity to consume." So complex are these systems that so far only gross approximations have resulted. The literature is voluminous on the work of the econometricians in this field but there does not appear to be an equivalent development in the ethical realm.

This does not mean, however, that control philosophy would not help those who work in the ethical fields. The fact that it is recognized that the free play of ethical forces is inadequate to insure optimum performance means that some kind of control is desirable. Parents face this ultimately in the ethical training of children. They also learn that the same control methods are not effective with children of different characters. The control that the Church exercised in England in the Middle Ages for a time was perhaps perfect for the system constraints under which it operated. The dynamics of the Tudor family somehow eluded analysis and another control system was substituted. This is not the place to attempt to extend control philosophy into the ramified areas of religion and psychology but there it no reason to assume that ethical control, optimized in accordance with formulae yet to be established, need be inconsistent with religion. The exercise might even contribute to religious unity.

While one cannot afford either too much or too little control (and just the right amount is something one determines from general principles), he never knows specifically what is needed until he has examined the specific system to be controlled. This can involve investigations of great complexity. For example, a governmental control problem should not be shrugged off on the basis that the philosophy of rugged individualism requires that we do not even consider external control nor should it be decided on the basis of bureaucratic edict. In spite of the fact that some of our solutions are plainly inadequate, the rational approach is often rejected for lack of time or patience. If so many people were not preoccupied with doing what machines can do better, such rationalizations as this might be carried out in more areas of public and private activity. The opportunities are inexhaustible. These are the things that only humans can do.

CHAPTER 12

AUTOMATION-AGE APOSTLES *CONTEMPLATIVUS IN ACTIONE*

by Rev. Thomas P. Gavigan, s.j., *Master of Novices, Novitiate of St. Isaac Jogues, Wernersville, Pennsylvania*

The Holy Father in his recent encyclical, *Mater et Magistra,* describes our era as one "penetrated and shot through with radical errors." The most radical of these, I presume, is secularism: the endeavor to live without God.

Historians of the future may characterize our age variously as the "Atomic Age," or the "Age of Anxiety," or the "Age of Automation," but it has one other characteristic which makes it stand out from all previous ages. It is a peculiarly God-less age. God is *out*—out of business, out of government, out of education, out of the relationship between the sexes. God is absent, banished, expelled from the major departments of modern life. Look at the number of our fellow citizens who are trying to lead genuine lives without God. Millions of them are trying to lay the foundations of their lives without their Creator. God has simply ceased to be an element in their lives. They live from day to day as if human life consisted merely in a skillful adaptation to the physical laws of nature, and as if death were the end of it. That is secularism. And, according to Mr. Will Herberg, it is really the religion of America today. We are no longer Protestant, Catholic or Jew. We Americans, he says, no matter what religion we profess, pretty well agree on what we consider the important things in life. And God, the things of God are not among them. We live in a society which concentrates on the patch of life between birth and death. That is what it is interested in. That is what all its energy is bent upon. Not only ordinary Christians but even religious can be affected by this viewpoint. If we are not careful, we can find ourselves thinking that the immediate things are the only things.

Father Danielou says that this is a particular danger to those of us who are interested in social problems. We object to the surface religion of many Catholics who reduce the Faith to certain practices and a purely individual moral code which stops short of social justice and charity. But we must be careful not to go to the other extreme of equating a social conscience and Christianity, like the college student who wrote: "Don't you think that a person who does not have the Faith, but who leads a blameless life and devotes himself whole-heartedly to social works has more of a chance of being saved than a person who leads a mediocre and selfish life, fulfilling the minimum obligations of the Catholic Faith?" Now it is perfectly true that love of one's neighbor is the touchstone of true love of God. But it is equally true that no amount of love of neighbor exempts one from the love of God. Rather, of the two commandments it is love of God which beyond any doubt is the first and greatest. The essence of our religion, *qua* religion, says Father Danielou, is not concern for others but man's acknowledgment of his dependence upon God. The relationship of man to God is essential to him as a human being. It is as essential as his relationship to other men. A man who does not pray, therefore, is not a man. He lacks something essential; he is in part mutilated. If I am here to utter truisms, let that be the first. It is the first and most fundamental reason for a prayer life. I have to make God's relation to me a reality. I have to keep the foundation truth in the fabric of my being, if I am going to be a man. And of course, this is all the more necessary, if I am to be a Christian and an apostle in this era. The main obstacle to a spiritual life today for religious as well as for others is the widespread preoccupation with material things. The remedy is that eminently immaterial thing—a prayer life.

St. Ignatius' ideal of what the prayer life of a Jesuit should be is summed up by Nadal in the well-known formulae: *"contemplativus in actione"* and "finding God in all things." In a passage describing some of Ignatius' mystical and extraordinary gifts of prayer, he says:

It is a fact that Father Ignatius received from God the particular grace of being able to rise without any effort to the contemplation of the Most Holy Trinity, and of reposing for a long period in that contemplation. Sometimes he was led by grace to contemplate the Trinity in its entirety; he was transported into it and united himself to it with his whole heart, with intense devotion and a profound spiritual relish.

Nadal continues: "But he was equally familiar with another type of prayer, which led him in all things, in every action to contemplate God present with a living awareness of spiritual realities—the contemplative in action, according to his maxim: 'in all things to find God.' " Of this latter privilege—finding God in all things—Nadal says: "What we have recognized here as a privilege of our Father Ignatius, we believe is given to the whole Society.

155

It is our belief that this gift . . . awaits all of us in the Society, and we declare boldly that it is part of our vocation."

There seems to be no doubt that in St. Ignatius this gift of finding God in all things was part of his mystical prayer, and as such really infused contemplation. But even in Ignatius' prayer we can distinguish a certain progression. After he entered upon a life "to help souls" he modified more and more not only his penance but also his prayer. Polanco notes this:

And when he was busy teaching Christian doctrine and at other works for the help of the neighbor which required a great deal of time, or at studies . . . he greatly shortened the time for prayer, and was satisfied with Mass, the examen of conscience, and about an hour for meditation. He thought it would be more acceptable to God our Lord for him to give more time and effort to the activities he undertook for God's service. The result was that despite the numerous difficulties he met with, he was during his studies one of the most zealous and hardest workers.

Chief among the difficulties in study for Ignatius was his tendency to experience special devotion and to become absorbed in prayer. Polanco notes again that "Ignatius studied with wonderful constancy . . . doing himself great violence, so as to be able to train under earthly masters a mind grown accustomed to a better Master, the Holy Spirit." This is not to say that during his life of study, Ignatius did not continue to apply himself to prayer. But the "great violence" which he had to do himself to limit his prayer, so as to be able to give himself entirely to work at hand, caused him to discover the spiritual way which was his own. Cut off from the consolation of immediate experience of God, he learned "to find God in all things." This is the way Ignatius himself characterizes the spiritual life of his last years: "He always grew in devotion, that is to say in the ease with which he found God, and more and more so now than ever in his whole life. Every time he wanted to find God, he found Him." Those around him noticed this. They remarked not only "his ease in uniting himself with God in prayer," but even more "the devotion he so easily felt in all things and in all places," being turned towards God even when he seemed at the time to be doing something else.

He had indeed come a long way from the seven hours of daily prayer he practiced at Manresa. Now his life was a continuous and spontaneous prayer, in which activity, far from disturbing his union with God, was the means of maintaining it. If we try to sum up this final stage in his spiritual development, we might call it "continual prayer in the midst of activity." In short, Ignatius found the perfection of his interior life in his apostolate.

When he began to train men in his company, he naturally taught them to follow the same way. This was the beginning of something completely new in the Church—a spirituality aimed at the active life of the apostle, a form of prayer ordered entirely to the active life. Heretofore the religious life was centered around contemplation and choir. So St. Ignatius' formula of finding God in all things not only gave the Society a unique piety, it was the inspiration for most modern religious communities, the secular institutes, and the whole idea of the lay apostolate, for it showed men how to combine union with God and the everyday duties of their state in life.

Naturally we are interested in this religious idea as it applies to us. A few quotations, I think, will suffice:

(1) Only a half year before his death, Ignatius wrote: "One must realize that man does not serve God only when he prays. Otherwise all prayer would be too

157

short. . . . But in reality, God is served better at certain times through other means than prayer, so that God is pleased if for this reason we omit prayer."

Ignatius, therefore, finds it quite all right that the apostolic worker does not have much time for formal prayer. Says Nadal: "He did not wish that the members of the Society seek God only in prayer but in all their actions, and that these be prayers. He approved this rather than long drawn-out contemplations."

(2) Polanco, writing in the name and under the eye of St. Ignatius to the Rector of a Scholasticate: "As to prayer and meditation, unless there is special need arising from troublesome and dangerous temptations . . . I see that our Father prefers that one try to find God in all that one does rather than devote a long time to prayer."

(3) To a priest who was in studies: "Concerning time for prayer, the answer is found in the purpose a scholastic in college has to pursue. His purpose is to acquire learning with which to serve God our Lord. If study is done well, it takes the whole person. One could not give whole-hearted attention to it, if he wanted long periods of prayer. What they can do after the prescribed spiritual duties is this: They should seek the presence of God our Lord in all things, for instance in association with others, in walking, looking, tasting, learning, thinking, indeed all they do."

(4) In the last ten years of his life, St. Ignatius carried on a running battle especially with the Spanish and Portuguese, who wanted to lengthen the time of prayer in the Society. When Nadal told him that

158

he had prescribed an hour and a half of prayer (as a compromise between the two hours the Spaniards wanted and the one hour Ignatius had appointed), St. Ignatius said that he could not be dissuaded from the conviction that for scholastics "one hour of prayer is enough where mortification and self-denial can be presumed to exist."

Now, I am sure that you have heard these and many other like quotations from both St. Ignatius and Nadal. It is clear that they describe an inner attitude of soul, a spiritual bent, which causes us to find God in the thick of work and activity. It is clear that this attitude of soul is a special grace (some hold that it is a gift of infused contemplation). Since it is a grace, we must pray often and confidently for it. But even though it is a grace of our vocation, from experience we know that it is not automatic. You do not acquire it by making a Long Retreat, or a Novitiate or Tertianship, or by living for years in the Society. There are no "easy steps" to it; so I won't try to detail any. Rather I should like to conclude by mentioning some of the means I think indispensable for disposing ourselves for this grace:

(1) Formal prayer at determined times. Without this the ideal of finding God in all things can remain a dangerous illusion. The faithful practice of prayer is a *sine qua non* for remaining united to God and finding Him in things. But it should be prayer with an apostolic viewpoint. We are not to look upon all activity as a "descent" or a "dissipation" *à la* Kempis. Nor are we to look on prayer as the period of building "spiritual capital," which is slowly spent in the course of the day's tasks and duties. Far from leading us away from prayer, our activity should awaken a fresh prayer, in which we

159

find God in what we are doing. Beginners, says St. Ignatius, need a period of training for this, and must pray "by certain rules and methods."

(2) Second means: Mortification and self-denial.

Again and again in his arguments against extending the time of prayer, Ignatius emphasizes the connection between finding God in all things and mortification and self-denial. Thus, in a letter to scholastics: "The truly mortified man who has conquered his passions finds in his prayer what he desires much more readily than a person who is not mortified and not striving for self mastery." You recall the saying of Ignatius: "Say not that he is a man of prayer, but rather that he is a mortified man." Recall, too, the remark already quoted: "for scholastics one hour of prayer is enough *where mortification and self-denial can be presumed to exist*."

(3) Third means: Seeking God's will in all things.

In his own life, to find the will of God was Ignatius' central concern. He never wanted to act according to his own will; he never wanted to do what appealed to him at the moment. He continually strove to discover what God wanted him to do in this particular situation. The search for the will of God is also central in the *Spiritual Exercises*. Their purpose: "to seek and find the will of God in the disposition of one's life." In the *Constitutions* and the *Letter on Obedience* St. Ignatius constantly enjoins us to see in the Superior the supreme authority of God, and hear in his command the will of God. Thus, for Ignatius, finding God in all things involves this interior conformity to God's will that is *perfect obedience*. It also involves the practice of the *pure intention* "not only in our state in life but in all its details."

For beginners, I am convinced that this is the most practical way—finding God by obedience and by purity of intention. Certainly it is more practical than trying to teach them contemplative union with Him in action, because it will produce the growth in unselfishness that must precede growth in prayer. Constant seeking of God's will, rather than acting on impulse and inclination, entails much self-denial; it entails as well much reflection and prayer. So, it is the best form of asceticism and active purification, which all the saints say are a *sine qua non*.

(4) Fourth means: Docility to the Holy Spirit.

We will succeed in seeing God in all things—in becoming contemplative in action—not by prayer alone or by action alone but by becoming holy. Now active holiness is not different from contemplative holiness. Holiness is the work of the Holy Spirit. And authors of all schools are at one on this: there is no achieving holiness except through the Holy Spirit. Certain means, certain methods, a certain pedagogy are common to both contemplative and apostolic holiness (I don't see how we can get around this): fidelity to prayer, a long period of asceticism, a constant seeking and doing of God's will, active and passive purifications, custody of heart and docility to the Holy Spirit.

For us, I think, the progress must be from selfless, reflective action to deeper prayer, after which prayer will inform and illumine action, making it possible to find God everywhere in the true contemplative sense. All of which, I admit, is much more easily said than done!

161

CHAPTER 13

AUTOMATION-AGE
APOSTLES
SECULAR INSTITUTES

by DR. JOHN J. O'CONNOR, *Professor of History, Georgetown University*

I WOULD LIKE TO speak briefly about three interrelated subjects:

> The Present Status of Christianity.
> Automation.
> Secular Institutes.

The present status of Christianity is a lowly one.

A colleague of mine at Georgetown University, Dr. U. S. Allers, recently directed a conference at the University on Christian Ethics and Nuclear Warfare.

He reminded the meeting that "Christianity and Christian values are not the dominant intellectual forces of our times. It is quite likely that at the critical moment the decisions will be made by men whose value commitments are basically non-Christian."

The Religious Editor of *The Detroit News*, Harold Schachern, wants to know why, after 2,000 years of Christianity, 1,917,000,000 persons, or 67.6 per cent of the population of the world, have never heard of Christ.

The 1960 *U. S. Catholic Overseas Missionary Personnel*

163

shows that there are now 6,782 persons serving as United States Catholic missionaries overseas, compared to 26,370 Protestants.

Out of 40,000,000 Catholic lay people, there are 178 lay people overseas.

In the concluding paragraphs of his 1961 pastoral letter for Lent, Richard Cardinal Cushing, Archbishop of Boston, said:

Christ's members are on the defensive in most places, on the decline in some, on the upgrade in only a few. Christianity, once the center of gravity of our civilization, is today a peripheral activity. At work, in leisure, in political, social, sexual, educational, professional, and family interests, the mass of the modern community is almost without trace of Christian values. The Church has great institutions and good organizations, but these represent partly an inheritance from the past and partly the energies of a minority within a minority.

The alienation or separation of the Church and society is not a new problem. This process of dissociation has been going on for centuries. It can be attributed to persecution —and to our own negligence.

A few years ago, the late Cardinal Suhard of Paris spoke of a long and wide wall which separates the Church and the city of men into two closed fields. Worship of God is the primary purpose of religion. But those who restrict it to that alone play into the hands of atheists.

This is what is happening today. Christianity is not getting much beyond the bounds of pious practices. Pius XII reminded us that the Gospel would never have been preached to the Japanese if Francis Xavier stayed in his room and prayed all day. Prayer must be joined with action.

This is the central issue of our time.

If there is any further alienation of the Church and society, if there is any further retreat into sanctuary, if our parishes become voluntary Catholic ghettoes, if we cultivate pious practices to the exclusion of concern for the appalling physical and moral condition of modern world society, then Communism will fill the ideological vacuum which we have permitted to occur, and the management of affairs will pass into the hands of those least qualified to solve the agonizing world crisis on any free, humane, or decent basis.

The mission of the Church today, in the words of Cardinal Montini, Archbishop of Milan, is that of bringing the sacred into a specific relation with the profane in such a way that Christianity will not be contaminated but communicated, and that modern society will not be deformed but sanctified.

Looking more closely at contemporary society, we find that certain profound changes are taking place.

According to Professor Irving Rosow of Western Reserve University, advances in science, technology, and automation introduce new skills so rapidly that occupational obsolescence comes at steadily younger ages. For years it has been difficult for men over forty to get industrial employment. However, technological developments now affect not only manual and less skilled workers, but reach into higher professional ranks and into the most advanced, complex branches of science as well.

In many fields a young engineering graduate has a useful life of about ten years before his knowledge is seriously outdated. He would have to spend up to a day each week in regular study just to stay abreast of current developments. And an experienced man might have to devote one-third of his time to self-education.

Similarly, an atomic physicist who enters industry with a doctor's degree at twenty-five needs a year's post-graduate study by the time he is forty in order to maintain his usefulness, his productivity, in the laboratory. Therefore, many corporations are now returning such scientists to the university for a year of post-graduate study at company expense.

The first challenge for the Catholic layman is obviously one of competence—a high degree of competence not only to stay abreast of developments but to rise to positions of leadership, influence, prestige, and authority in the various fields of human endeavor.

I am fully aware that the achievement of competence—and the driving motivation behind it—is a bothersome problem and has given concern to Jesuit educators for many months in all parts of the United States. I am merely suggesting here one avenue of approach—the religious approach, the concept of an intellectual apostolate.

Last summer I had a long talk in Dublin with Frank Duff, founder of the worldwide Legion of Mary. His idea is that the Catholic layman must be the very best in his vocation, whatever it may be, in the arts as well as in the sciences.

But the long-delayed Christian reconstruction of society not only requires professional and technical competence of a high order, in the whole range and gamut of the layman's working life, but also positive Christian guidelines of action.

In this respect we are most fortunate in having as our textbook of social advance and improvement the recent great encyclical of Pope John XXIII entitled *Mater et Magistra*.

The final problem is this: How do we propose to go about reducing the splendor of the Church's teaching to specific programs of concrete action?

A few days ago, I was talking to a young man, a member of a secular institute called Opus Dei. He told me that

166

at the present time, two hundred and sixty professionally trained young laymen, graduates of leading universities in forty countries—physicians, engineers, lawyers, chemists, space-scientists, university professors—are devoting several years of their lives to the study of ecclesiastical subjects in the academic Center of Opus Dei, the Roman College of the Holy Cross, and in the various Pontifical Universities of the Eternal City.

These young men are combining a solid professional and technical training with a thorough doctrinal and religious formation that is designed to complete the development of their personalities to the greatest possible extent.

Some of the young men will be ordained priests. But the vast majority of them will return to their native countries and practice their professions. Even the priests will be associated with those in their former professions and can be expected to have a great influence because they will know intimately the opportunities and problems of those professions.

The high effectiveness of this rigorous training, professional and ecclesiastical, is indicated by the fact that one of these young lay graduates, twenty-eight years old, has established, almost single-handedly, a new college in Kenya, East Africa. It is called Strathmore College, and it is an interracial college. This is a new forward thrust in education and, simultaneously, a new forward thrust in interracial relations in Africa.

Secular institutes such as Opus Dei are a providential answer to contemporary social problems for two basic reasons: they provide a powerful incentive to the layman to achieve a high degree of technical competence in his work, and they provide excellent training facilities for the development of sanctity.

We cannot transform society from the inside, so to

167

speak, unless we are at the social, economic, political, scientific, and educational heart of things in roles of leadership and responsibility.

The man who will exercise maximum influence in urban renewal, for example, is the man who is conducting, directing, and supervising day-by-day operations in the field of urban renewal.

It is likewise true that we cannot hope to transform present-day society unless the professional and technical specialists are also men and women who are forever striving for a closer union with Christ, who possess a strong, deep, profound spiritual and moral formation.

There are two kinds of laymen—the passive dolt and the apostle. Secular institutes train apostles.

There are two categories of the lay apostolate: the first, concerned principally with the City of God, is bound up closely with the direct apostolate of the Church; the second, concerned principally with the City of Man, is bound up closely with the things of Caesar and this world.

In the first category, Pope Pius XII spoke of catechists, teachers, and those engaged in youth work. With respect to the second category, the Holy Father said that the relations between the Church and the world require the intervention of lay apostles. The *"consecratio mundi"* is essentially the work of laymen themselves, of men who are intimately a part of economic and social life.

There is a great need today for lay apostles in both categories. Secular Institutes train laymen and laywomen in both categories.

The two realms of lay activity are not mutually exclusive. Rather they complement each other. I have taken part in both categories of the lay apostolate. For many years I was a member of the Catholic Evidence Guild and taught Christian Doctrine in the public parks of Washington. My major concern today is with the City of Man, with race relations, with the values and institutions of temporal society, with community and civic responsibility.

The same layman, of course, can teach Confraternity of Christian Doctrine classes in his parish and also be a member of a Catholic Interracial Council. Generally speaking, the man who is interested in Papal Volunteers for Latin America is not interested in the Peace Corps, and the Peace Corps agricultural specialist is not interested in teaching catechism. Secular institutes are an answer to both interests and both needs.

Secular institutes provide an ingredient that so many lay enterprises lack; namely, stability and/or permanence.

Secular institutes are an answer to the clergy-laity relationship because a lawyer-priest has a very practical understanding of the lawyer-layman. There is no problem of communication.

Secular institutes make it possible for laymen to pursue their ecclesiastical studies slowly and at different periods, or simultaneously with their university or professional work. In this way, provision is made for an integral formation which is complete in all five aspects: human, ascetic, professional, theological, and apostolic. This kind of training lends itself to a thorough integration of speculative and practical knowledge.

But the real uniqueness of secular institutes is that, for the first time in its history, the Church has admitted lay people to a juridically recognized state of perfection.

The basic documents are *Provida Mater Ecclesia,* the Apostolic Constitution concerning canonical states and secular institutes directed to the attainment of Christian perfection, issued by Pope Pius XII in 1947; a *Motu Propio, Primo Feliciter,* in praise of secular institutes and in confirmation thereof, issued by Pius XII in 1948; and

169

an Instruction on secular institutes from the Sacred Congregation of Religious, entitled *Cum Sanctissimus,* and
issued in 1948.

Pius XII has defined secular institutes as "societies,
whether clerical or lay, whose members, in order to attain
Christian perfection and to exercise a full apostolate, profess the evangelical counsels in the world."

Members of a secular institute keep the personal status
they enjoyed before entering the institute; they remain lay
persons or clerics. They are not required to lead a common life or to observe the canonical laws of the cloister.
The lay people do not wear an ecclesiastical garb. They
take only private vows of poverty, chastity, and obedience.
The Holy See requires that there be a common house for
administration purposes, religious formation, and the care
of sick and aged members. Bishops have the right to found
secular institutes after consultation with the Sacred Congregation for Religious.

Existing lay groups can be developed as pious unions or
confraternities before seeking approval as secular institutes. Persons desiring membership in an institute, in addition to practicing those exercises of piety and self-denial
which all must practice who aspire to the perfection of
Christian life, must effectively tend toward that same perfection also in the following three special ways:

(1) By making profession before God of celibacy and
perfect chastity, which shall be confirmed by vow,
oath, or consecration binding in conscience;

(2) By a vow or promise of obedience, so that they dedi-
cate themselves entirely to God and to works of
charity or apostleship by a stable bond, and are
always in all respects morally in the hands and under the guidance of their superiors;

(3) By a vow or promise of poverty, in virtue of which they have not the free use of temporal property but a restricted and limited use.

A life of perfection, a bond of unity, an apostolic object or purpose, a secular character and a certain amount of progress or maturity—these are the requisites for a secular institute. Married people can be associated with an institute and may even take the vows or promises of poverty, chastity and obedience to be practiced according to their state of life.

Let me say for the record that I am not a member of any secular institute. But I have been for some years a cooperator or associate of Opus Dei.

The Secretary General of Opus Dei, Alvaro del Portillo, stated a few years ago that the number of secular institutes in the Church was forty-nine. Of these, twelve were of pontifical right and thirty-seven of diocesan right. The institutes for men numbered thirteen (seven sacerdotal and six lay), while the remaining thirty-six were for women.

Applications from Associations (Pious Unions, Sodalities, Confraternities, Third Orders) received by the Sacred Congregation of Religious to become secular institutes amounted to one hundred and ninety-seven.

The figures of one hundred and ninety-seven applications and forty-nine approved institutes refer to the period of eleven years, from February 2, 1947, the date of the promulgation of the Apostolic Constitution, *Provida Mater Ecclesia,* to the end of 1957.

The forty-nine institutes so far approved have been founded in the following countries: Austria, two; Belgium, one; Canada, one; Colombia, two; England, one; France, seven; Germany, two; Italy, twenty-one; Mexico, one; Spain, seven; Switzerland, two; Uruguay, one; Yugoslavia, one.

Are secular institutes making progress in the United States?

Father Walter M. Abbott, S.J., Associate Editor of *America*, gave a report on secular institutes in the issue of May 20, 1961. In the report itself he stated that in the United States today there are twenty that have been canonically established. Eight other groups are on the way to the basic official status of "approved pious associations," from which they can move on to the ranks of fully approved secular institutes. A number of other Catholic lay organizations may soon take the same route to total dedication in the world.

In the chart accompanying the report, entitled "Secular Institutes in the United States," Father Abbott gives the following breakdown:

(1) Institutes of Papal Law: 8
(2) Institutes of Diocesan Law: 3
(3) Approved Associations: 6
(4) Potential Institutes: 8
                                  ——
                                  25

I don't know how to reconcile the figures in the report (twenty canonically-established and eight other groups on the way to official status for a total of twenty-eight) with the chart which gives a total of 25; two of the approved associations have their headquarters in Canada.

There is no indication in Father Abbott's report as to which secular institutes are branches or extensions of European institutes and which are of American origin. I think we can say, briefly, that there are about two dozen secular institutes in the United States today. Generally speaking, the growth of secular institutes in the United States has not matched their development in other countries.

Secular institutes thus far established encourage adoration of the Blessed Sacrament in parish churches, publish and distribute ascetic works, foster the liturgical apostolate, establish and maintain protective organizations for working girls, services, houses, and places of religious instruction. They give assistance to the poor and sick in their homes. They do parish work, settlement house work, work in special schools and institutions for the underprivileged, and such specialized work as the conversion of non-Catholics.

Many of these activities are familiar to most Catholics. What particularly fascinates me is that Opus Dei has more than two hundred student residences around the world and that two hundred and sixty professionally trained laymen are studying ecclesiastical subjects in Rome.

The long-range impact of secular institutes, as I see it, will be to act as a leaven in the mass in two respects: to improve the low quality of Catholic life in the age of automation, and to influence, in a profound way, the social values and institutions in the City of Man by a combination of strong intelligence and great love.

CHAPTER 14

AUTOMATION IN
THE LIFE OF A CATHOLIC

by REV. GUSTAVE WEIGEL, S.J., *Professor of Ecclesiology, Woodstock College*

I BELIEVE THAT quite literally this particular conference is an afterthought of the organizers of this seminar. It is not surprising that in a theologate the speculative theological position on man and his history would be overlooked. After all, theology is no prophet in its own country. But we must remember that there is such a thing as a theological cosmology, a theological consideration and vision of the world and man.

I wish to speak to you about automation, of which I know almost nothing, from the point of view of a theologian which exempts him from knowing much about it. And in order to do so, I wish to propose right in the beginning three postulates which are taken from theology.

The first postulate is a dogmatic doctrine of the Church. The Church insists that the cosmic order is bidimensional, the natural dimension and the supernatural. These two orders are strictly dimensions. They are not two things hermetically sealed off one from the other. The supernatural supposes the natural. The supernatural is in the natural, elevating it. We have, therefore, from this dogmatic principle the basic position for a Catholic: namely, that we are in a world which is bidimensional, one dimension natural

175

and the second dimension supernaturally rooted in it and infused with it.

Now this first principle is extraordinarily important for Catholics who wish to work in natural society and deal with the problems which arise from economics in such a society. The second principle, which is also dogmatic and given to us in the Council of Trent, is that the natural order in relation to man is under the blight of original sin. Any dynamism, therefore, that can be found in the things of nature will always thwart man's desire. Let me repeat, will *always* thwart man's desire. Anything that man can envision as a beautiful human situation cannot be produced by the powers in nature.

Catholic dogma insists, however, that this principle should not be exaggerated. The Council of Trent rejected all forms of total depravity. The natural order did not lose the original goodness, which the Creator saw in it (Gen. 2:31). It did, however, as St. Paul brings out, lose its original justice—a better translation is "original rightness." The power indeed is there and the power is by its own native origin good. But a perverting demonic force, called in John's Gospel the Prince of this World, will always cripple and deviate the power which is in nature, that power which man uses in order to satisfy as far as he can his own dreams and needs. We must take this principle very seriously. If we do not, our plannings would certainly become delusions. There is no way this side of the Day of the Lord to harness the powers which indeed are at our disposal to produce the new heavens and the new earth. They will be produced indeed in the Day of the Lord, but it will require Divine Power to bring it about.

The third postulate I borrow from Teilhard de Chardin. Let's call it a physico-theological principle. As Teilhard saw it, cosmic reality, which is coarse, finite, material reality, is a manifold of countless instances. It is one thing, but shows up in many ways, and all these instances are inextricably interwoven. You find the power at work in everything about us, and every action influences every other action.

In this movement, and there is nothing static in it, you will find a push being made in every possible direction to create a bigger and better organization of the powers which are at hand. It moves out in all directions until at one point on the diameter it can move upward, and there begins the spiral once more, moving ever upward, and it moves upward to a higher degree of intellectuality.

Matter, as we know it, is indeed subject to the law of thermodynamic deterioration, but that deterioration is strictly on the external level of matter's *actio ad extra.* There is also a radial energy which is *ad intra,* and this radial energy produces the higher form of intellectuality. It is precisely by this inner intellectualism that the movement of matter, which is one homogeneous thing, takes on greater momentum and, in its acceleration, can make itself transparent so that through it can be dimly seen the Creator who moves it by His presence. In its own progressive evolution, a point will be reached when God can be seen in all. The movement, therefore, of the material is to hominification—to use a word very like the one coined by Teilhard de Chardin. In this hominification, the movement is to ever greater transparency of the world's stuff so that in it can be seen the Power which is Divinity.

For Teilhard, although man has already appeared on this earth and perhaps elsewhere too, the process is not yet finished. Evolution is still going on even in man. There is no question of producing an individual man. What must be produced is a species-subject, a new social form, whereby even in man's action we will see reflected the principle of the Trinity where all of the actions of God outwards from the Godhead Itself are of One Agent. *Ac-*

tiones ad extra sunt unius Dei. The Three Persons work in complete and utter cooperation and collaboration. There is no possibility of isolation of these Three Persons in the single, unified, divine action.

I accept this vision of Teilhard de Chardin as a postulate; so I have three: the existence of a double order, natural and supernatural; secondly, the existence of a demonic force perverting the good in the natural order. This demonic force is called by John the Prince of this World and by theologians in general, the principle of original sin. The third postulate is that in the cosmos on which we live we find an evolution, a natural evolution, moving from a tremendous chaotic origin to an ever more intellectualized movement, going to a point which Teilhard de Chardin called the Omega Point, and there, when that point is reached, Power Itself, God, will be seen all in all.

Those are the postulates. Let's draw some corollaries that should be helpful for you in your discussion. Although they will solve none of your questions, they will certainly help you to avoid the possibility of making wrong answers to possibly wrong questions. In order that we may have this evolution of the cosmos, it is necessary that man, the rational, material creature wherever he is to be found—on this earth or in other celestial bodies makes no difference—have control of power. Perhaps if I give you an image, you may appreciate somewhat this notion which must be basic in your theological thinking. Conceive our cosmic reality as ooze, black and dark, moving in a slithery, contorted fashion, and in this slithery, contorted movement, it moves around a Vortex. It is percisely because of the presence of the Vortex that movement dwells in this dull, slow, opaque stuff. If I can move it faster, if I can make it whip around that Vortex so that it itself becomes thinner, I can whip it finally to the state where in its movement I can see through it and see the heart of the real.

We need not be surprised that this writhing stuff, this slithery slime, does not of itself have within it the power and the drive to become transparent. It is the presence of the Vortex that brings about that movement. It is by reason of the Vortex that this lethargic mass has any dynamism or mobility. We cannot, therefore, look into cosmic reality itself for its meaning. Its meaning is to make clear and apparent the Vortex energy which actually is making this world live and move.

Evolution, therefore, is the very essence of the being of anything that is finite. Creation is evolving; its being is to change by reason of its nearness to the Divine Power. The more it moves, the greater will be the demand for more acceleration. This movement, by reason of the principle of original sin, will go on because the movement is not bad, but the movement will never be able to move in the line of reason, in the line of pure intellectualism, because of the presence of the Prince of this World, that perverting principle which will always drive a good thing toward wrong goals. It is a misdirection which is at work in something which of itself is indeed quite good, and yet this very movement of perversion within this opaque, slithery mass is not without its own evolutionary contribution. The movement will take place, and in the perverting movement, action will result, and in this action, we are accelerating toward the Day of the Lord, the *Parousia,* when He will come to us and then make the new heavens and the new earth. That day will not be made by evolution. It will have to be made by God who made that which is evolving to become, when He puts His hand in it, a new world where the heart of man will be satisfied, where his hunger for justice and for fraternity will be sated.

If this be true, as Teilhard de Chardin supposed, our evolution at the present moment is to an ever greater solidarity of mankind. We are moving to become a single species-subject of action. Individuals can no longer consider themselves in isolation. In the stage of evolution in which we have entered, all individuals become closer in action and being to all other individuals. Yet we have this evolutionary movement in us to bring us all together, subject to the power of the demonic force which is disintegrating.

Man, in order to live up to his natural, peremptory nisus to bring the black stuff of material reality to ever greater transparency, must exploit physical power, and he is always in search of greater physical power.

Automation is a new beginning, not, by any means, the end of the employment of ever greater and greater power. Man, as he showed up first on this earthly stage, depended on human muscle as the source of energy. Because this was his sole source, you had slavery. Men were used precisely as economic forces and nothing else. As knowledge grew, men learned to domesticate animals, but it was still biological muscle which acted as the main source of energy, as the source whereby man could create. Man could move the opaque mass of cosmic reality a bit faster.

Through the thousands and thousands of years of his existence, man gradually learned to use the sun, at least to give him light and heat. He also used the wind, and we know that by using it he could sail his ships. He used the running water which made mills run. He used gravity in the form of falling weights. These were newer and richer sources of energy. In the last century, he finally moved on to steam. Yet steam requires coal, oil, and water. From then and from there, he quickly moved to the internal combustion machine which exploited a limited supply of petroleum. In all this economic evolution, what was man doing? He was only exploiting the different, complex configurations in which cosmic energy expresses itself.

180

It was given to our time to show that the very heart of matter in its simplest form is power, and today we use atomic radiation. It is a new beginning. This form of energy exploitation will evolve yet more, and no man now can see the end of all that it can do. We are, therefore, in a new era. This has been seen by many men of our century. The difference between the world of radioactive power, of the tapping of the atom, from, let us say, the age of Thomas Aquinas, is so utterly great that we can almost say that qualitatively these two worlds are different.

But let us get one thing clear. With this new source of energy available to us, we are dealing with something cosmic, and we are, therefore, dealing with something which is under the dominance of the perverting principle of the Prince of this World. You cannot screen him out. He is part and parcel of it. He will indeed be thrown out, but that will be in the Day of the Lord.

Now what are the fruits of the perversion introduced by this demonic force? Injustice, cruelty, intemperance, ambition, inhumanity. You are not going to order these things out of a world just because you are using atomic energy. You cannot lift yourself up by your bootstraps. Before the coming of the *Parousia,* the Prince of this World will still be active and be dominant. Do not make plans, therefore, in which you promise us paradise. As a theologian, I can tell you that you can't make it. And if your plan is meant to give me Eden, there is something wrong with your plan. It is, of course, true that in the older systems of power exploitation you had sin and vile vices show up in the degree in which they could in such a framework. Much of that will disappear, but there will be new forms in which they will manifest themselves, forms perhaps that we today cannot yet envision.

What shall we do about them? First of all, *we* won't be

around, so we don't have to do anything. Secondly, in their limited fashion, moralists of those days will try to handle these problems.

In this world, moving on to ever greater availability of power, moving on to an ever more accelerated momentum and creativity, perverted indeed as it is by the Prince of this World, there is a supernatural human society. This human society was introduced by God's mercy and grace to give unto men, even within the slithery, contorted action of the opaque stuff which we call cosmic reality, peace, a peace such as the world does not know, and it is a society, a solidarity, a union of men. It is open, open for all, but not all will enter. Only those will enter who in faith love God, who in the strange experience of faith attach themselves to that which they do not see and cling in hope to the Vortex which, of course, appears as nothing.

This society, which is the Church, is put right into the world. It is not removed from it. The Founder of this Church, Christ, said that it would act as a leaven in the mass, the opaque mass. This Church knows about evolution It, too, evolves. St. Paul tells us that it will evolve until the moment when it has reached the full stature of Christ, that moment when it will have within itself in the union of an organism, all those whose names are written in the Book of Life. It must, therefore, evolve. It does evolve. And it evolves not of itself alone but in terms of the evolution of the natural order. They are interfused. The evolution of the natural order helps to bring about the evolution of the Church, to make her grow to the full stature of Christ.

Some men of the Church, in the past and the present (and I am quite sure in the future likewise), try to stop evolution. They would like to freeze it. "If Thomas wrote, no one need write again. He said it all. All moral problems have been solved by us; all you have to do is go back to the books of Busenbaum." But these men are not thinking with the Church. These are men who do not understand that the life of the Church is growth and evolution, conditioned and spurred on by the natural evolution which is the law of the cosmos.

There is, however, this difference between the two evolutionary actions. Under the pervertive power of the Prince of this World, men try to evolve the world into ever greater and greater creativity for its own sake in order to be satisfied with what nature can give us. The Church is quite different. It does not object to evolution. It is all for it because this is the dynamic part of its being. But it wants to see the true end of all evolution, which means making things transparent so that in seeing them I no more see them than I see the glasses which I wear, but through them, I see the reality which is soul-satisfying, which will bring peace, justice, and a helpful, completely edifying form of human solidarity. It is not a question, therefore, of evolution against nonevolution. Both nature and supernature cling to the evolutionary being which is their own. But the Church wants to see it in terms of the *Logos,* the *Logos* become Flesh, the *Logos* through which all things were made and without which nothing was made. We cling to the enfleshed *Logos* to show us what the world means. In so doing, the world itself will be a pedagogue leading us to the mysteriously satisfying inner Vortex.

To prophesy is, of course, something that men are prone to do. Never be afraid to make prophecies. Men expect prophecies to fail, and therefore, when they are not realized, no one is surprised. If you do prophesy truly, people remember and call you wise. Yet we cannot prophesy infallibly about the details of the world which automation is beginning to give us. But this we can say in the light of the postulates with which I began. Substantially the human situation is going to be as it was in the past. The greater power released through man's intelligence will make him ever more and more impressed and dazzled by power itself. It is power which he adores, but the Christian will not adore it if it is finite. The Christian will see that such power is itself only a product of mercy, love, and justice, and he knows that mercy, love, and justice are present in us through Christ, the Lord.

We will have in the future what we have had in the past: the choice between Christolatry and idolatry. Those who in faith believe that the *Logos* is God Incarnate, that He is the Vortex jumping over into the opaque, slithery, writhing mass, will adore Him. The others will adore mere power which they do not even know how to hypostatize and, therefore, will adore that which is only a product of God who is Mercy, Love, and Justice.

The Prince of this World will see to it that this be done. As Catholics, we cannot get rid of him. We can keep him out of our own fraternity to some degree. He will not be able to destroy the House of Christ, for this power is not given to him. But he will certainly attack the Christion of this new world living ever more closely with all the human beings in the world, becoming every day not so much the individual artist, the individual craftsman, but mainly an element in a composite subject of creation. When the Christian feels and sees this, he will necessarily have problems greater than we have known to date.

I have always found that those who preach fraternity and social solidarity can do it best if they are far from the teeming herd. Living with a brother, in the close proximity of fraternity, produces for both brothers a certain amount of friction when they are so close to each other's smell, and this is not necesssarily perfume. This will be a problem for the future Christian, a problem of charity in which he believes. How this charity can be worked out will be, of course, the problem of the future Church. Rules will be made. They will only be human rules, and, therefore, men cannot expect from them too much. But they will manifest that which is our Faith: namely, the need of love of man for man because man loves God-made-Man.

And these rules, no matter how imperfectly they work out, will be an act of faith. I believe that the real problem with the age of automation as it will develop more and more, will be the question of faith itself. The temptation of the Christian will not be the same as it was two thousand years ago for the very simple reason that the process of being pushed together, one toward the other, will demand a life more disciplined than when there was more room between men. Certain types of indiscipline which can be vicious probably will not be possible in those days. But the question of faith will certainly arise. Cosmic power will be released. An ever wider and wider horizon of power and its use will be seen by man. He will move from this little earth out into the uncounted bodies in the heavens, and he will feel himself to be God Himself.

For the Christian faced with this tremendous power and with its dazzling product, it will be a matter of constant effort to renew his act of belief. It is perhaps not without its sad poignancy that when Christ spoke of the Day of the Lord, with all the apocalyptic images proper to that kind of utterance, He put in the little phrase, "When the Son of Man comes, will He find, do you think, faith upon the earth?" (Luke 18:8).

CHAPTER 15

A CONSERVATIVE
VIEWS AUTOMATION

by BARRY M. GOLDWATER, *U. S. Senator*
(R) from Arizona

IN MY OWN personal opinion, automation is not only a must for the United States. As we go into the 1960s, it constitutes one of our greatest economic and social problems. By virtue of wage contracts, negotiations, minimum wage, etc., we have, in effect, priced ourselves to a level that we might say is out of the competitive area of world trade. Now there is only one way by which we are going to regain and retain our position in world commerce, and that is by making sure that in this country each hour spent in production produces more. When we, for example, pay $2.62 an hour plus bonuses in the copper industry, and want to compete with Chile that pays $2.50 a day, or Peru that pays $2.70 a day, or Africa that pays $16.75 a week, there is only one answer. We have to cause the hourly wage that we pay to produce more so that the unit production cost will come down. We do that by mechanizing so that the man himself has less to do.

Now this holds true all through industry. I don't care where we look. Automation can be applied, and automation will be applied, to regain our competitive position in the world. We are faced with an example in the automotive field. A few years ago, we exported as many as a hundred thousand passenger cars a year. But last year we exported only about eight thousand and imported about a hundred thousand. The reason was not just price; it was quality too. I am thinking of the Mercedes-Benz in which, if you look carefully, you will find all screwheads aligned. They just don't quit turning the screw when it is at right angles. They will run them perpendicular and all will be the same. And these cars run and run and run with no trouble. And our cars run and run and run, and they are a dream to the repairmen.

Now we can offset that to a large extent by more automation. We already have to some extent. The automobile industry is a very highly automated industry, but more is needed.

My brother and I run a chain of women's and children's stores that might be compared to Garfinkels in Washington, although it is not so large. In our business we have about seven hundred employees. This very afternoon, it would be possible for us to replace sixty of these people by putting in coin machines. For example, why is it necessary for a person to wait on a customer who merely wants a white handkerchief or a pair of socks or a cake of soap or a tube of shaving cream or a toothbrush? These are items which one picks up on the way home. You could drop a quarter, a dollar, or two dollars into a machine and get what you wanted.

Now the big problem arises. What do we do with the sixty people? We are not hardhearted employers in this country, in spite of what some labor leaders would have you think. Here is a corporation, mine for example, that could make more money by having fewer people. But we know that if we turn these people loose, they will become a drag on society. Most of these people are elderly, or they are young girls waiting to get married. So we retain them.

But as taxes mount, as the profit picture becomes smaller and smaller, businesses will be forced into this position. In my own business, we find a good example. When I went to work over 30 years ago, a 10 per cent profit in the mercantile business was not unheard of. In fact if you made less than 10 per cent, you were playing too much pinochle or—we didn't play gin rummy then—pool. But today if you make 2½ per cent, people come to your store from all over the country to see what you do to effect savings whereby you can make that kind of profit.

There is no sign at all that government expenditures are going to decrease. And there is every sign that taxes will increase, that government will get bigger, that bureaucracy will grow, that regulation of business will come to the point where even staying in business will be a challenge. So we are faced with many factors that force automation, and automation, as I say, must come.

In this country today, according to a study made by McGraw-Hill, there is somewhere around ninety to ninety-five billion dollars worth of obsolete machinery. This machinery will not be replaced until a proper depreciation or write-off allowance is put into the tax code. The president has suggested $1,700,000,000 credit. That is like throwing a glass of water on a fire that might consume this whole building. It actually favors a new business more than an old one. In April I asked the head of one of our large steel companies what he spent for new machinery. He said that industry would spend $670,000,000 tomorrow if it could get a liberal write-off allowance.

Now of the eight leading economies in the world, we are the slowest. I am not too concerned about that because the other seven were devasted by war. If they were not maintaining a growth rate of between 3 to 7½ or 8 per cent, we would be in trouble because they would be in trouble. But they are growing faster than we are, and we

189

have the most rigid depreciation allowances of any country in the world. Depreciation, as you know, is something
that allows you to write off a piece of machinery. In our
country it stretches out over twenty years. The danger
is that you buy a lathe today for five thousand dollars,
in twenty years, the way we are going, we can almost be
certain that this lathe will cost twenty thousand dollars.
But if you could write that lathe off in a year or two or
three, then you would have the money to replace it or
even to buy another one. You would be buying it at a
very slight increase and instead of paying taxes on one
piece of equipment you would actually be paying taxes on
two. There are, therefore, many advantages in this approach.

The biggest advantage would be, I am convinced, that
if the president asked this afternoon for a completely liberalized depreciation allowance to the point that a business man could almost make up his own system, within a
month we would run into a manpower shortage in this
country. The mere fact that people would put in orders
for machinery that they do not have—people who are
now going to Europe to buy these machines and who place
them in Europe—would stay in this country. It would put
every unemployed man who wanted to work back at work,
and we would actually find, as Germany is finding, a manpower shortage. Just recently, the Volkswagen people
bought Germany's largest bicycle plant. Why? To build
bicycles? No. They quit building bicycles. They put every
man to work building automobiles because they did not
have enough people.

If this were done, this economy would, in my opinion,
start growing at a rate of nearly 4 per cent. It might ex-
ceed that. I am not one of those wild-eyed business men
who think that we can get up to 5 or 6 per cent as a constant factor. But we would certainly get up to around

4 per cent, which would show us an economy the likes of which we have never had.

But, of course, this does create a great social problem, and we cannot forget it. Now let me try to convince you that the American businessman is no longer the hard-hearted man such as was found back in the twenties. That man did not care whether you worked or not as long as he made his buck. Today you will find the average business-man as socially-minded as anybody else. He is concerned about his employees. He knows that if his employee goes out of work, he himself will pay part of his support through taxes, through charity, through donations to his church or fraternal organizations. So he wants to keep that person either working for him or gainfully employed elsewhere.

There are many approaches to this problem. Of course, the whole approach is education. What do you do with the woman who is put out of work at Goldwater's, let's say, because we put in a vending machine to vend cosmetics? It should be our responsibility to train her, if we can, to do some other job in our business. It would be to our advantage because she has our interest at heart. She has worked with us; she knows our systems. And we are trying to do just that as much as we can. Where we cannot find a place for her in our own operation, there is a possibility that we might train her to the point where she could get a job someplace else.

The other day in the Labor and Public Welfare Committee, a bill was unanimously reported by Republicans and Democrats alike that would provide money for job training for people who are out of work. Actually you might say it is an upgrading of the vocational training system. Where vocational training is primarily interested in the skills of the hand—welding, lathe work, metal work, wood work—this would go past that into accounting, even dressmaking design, pattern work, and other things. People are being displaced. In this country a large number of these people are unemployed because of automation, and again this is a very natural thing and I am sorry that government did not recognize the possibility of it happening sooner.

Let us imagine that you are running a business. From 1940 until about 1955, we went through a wartime economy where almost anything went. If you did not make money, you were goofing off. People came into your place of business and said, "I want this," or "I want that." We did not require salesmanship. True, you could not have used sloppy methods of bookkeeping or management, but you did not have to be so meticulous as you do now. In my estimation, the wartime economy ended in 1955. We had by that time developed the military firepower per man capability to the point that we did not need so many men in the field and we did not need so many men in the factory, building the weapons for those men. So today, the war effort is costing less than 9 per cent of our total production, where during the war it was costing us 44 per cent. We have, therefore, the problem now of factories like Martin, Boeing, Lockheed and others having to lay men off because they actually are not needed anymore to turn out the weapons that we once had to have.

In business, as these dips come along now and then, you find that they are merely inventory adjustments and that there is nothing new, startling, or unusual about them. Any man in business expects to go through a periodic leveling off of business or an actual dip in business where he adjusts his inventory. If it gets too high, he cleans out his inventory by sale. The public gets a little more picayunish about quality. I think that is one of the troubles today. The American public is asking for more for its money and they are not getting it. Frankly, they are not getting their dollar's worth, in my estimation, in every case. Then you have a period of slump.

What do you do as a business man? You have to stay in business. That is your first duty to yourself, your employees, and your stockholders. You begin looking around the shop to see where you can put a machine that might eliminate a part of your payroll, payroll being the largest chunk of a man's expense. In fact, in my particular business, the payroll is 60 per cent of the expense dollar, and in the factories it will run as high as 80 per cent. So you find a machine that does this job just as well as Sally and Mary can do it, and you let Sally and Mary go. But Sally and Mary do not get their jobs back when you come out of the slump. This, mind you, is what has happened in the last two adjustment periods where we now find unemployment on a seasonally adjusted basis of nearly 6 per cent and a straight unadjusted basis of around 6½ per cent. It is not caused by the fact that these men do not want to go to work. The jobs in which they have been skilled are filled, or a machine has already displaced them. You are going to see more and more and more of this situation as the American businessman, who actually wants to stay in business in this country, buys more and more machinery.

The United States Steel Company pulls its wire in Birmingham, Alabama, on machinery that was put in a plant in 1895. You can imagine what they can pull on 1895 machinery. So now they pull it in Belgium because it can be done more cheaply. In fact, all the barbed wire that we buy now for our western cattle ranges is made in Belgium and distributed through our largest barbed wire manufacturer in the United States—only because of the difference in cost and the fact that he has not automated yet.

This social problem is going to be cured in only one

193

way, and that is by education. Now I personally feel that it should be an effort made by business and labor. But the government has its nose in the tent as it does every time a problem arises. We have a bill out that will let government finance this educational effort completely for two years and then on a 50 per cent matching basis with the states. I still think that it would be better if the business man himself engaged in this because he would then get closer to the real social needs of people, and people would no longer be merely a number on his total payroll. I see, therefore, in the coming decades—in fact I think in the 1960s—a much more rapid use of automation forming our chief social and economic headache. And I must say that without complete automation of America's factories, we are not going to catch up with foreign competition. We cannot expect to cut our wages back. We do not want to do that, although I must say that they would do just that in Europe because wages there are what we call real money wages—in other words, how much the man is taking home, not how many dollars or how many francs or how many pounds, but what will it buy. And as it becomes necessary to adjust that purchasing power, the salary is decreased in order to keep the purchasing power normal. That sounds kind of silly, but if you have the dollar decreasing in value, you are going to find the cost of living increasing as we are finding in this country. But we are not of that type. We Americans do not suggest that because we are in a competitive position that our $3.00-an-hour steelworker take less, even though a group in West Virginia said not so long ago that they would rather be working at $1.50 an hour than not working at $3.00 an hour.

So automation is our answer. And I think that as we proceed we will see completely automated factories in

194

order that the $3.00-an-hour wage that we pay will produce $3.00 an hour.

And in coming to the end of my remarks let me say this: I do not blame the labor leader for constantly wanting to get an increase for his men. That is part of his job. That is like the politician: if he does not get something for his people at home, he does not get reelected. But doing this has placed the average American product out of competition with the foreign market. We have given wage increases in this country that are not compatible with productivity increases. Productivity is a difficult thing to measure in many, many instances, but it is not hard to measure where a man is turning out so many things an hour with his hands. If he is not turning out enough to earn that $3.00, you have to absorb part of that $3.00 in an increased price. Then you are doing harm to the whole economy. If he is doing enough to earn that $3.00, in fact if he is doing more, then by all means that man, that individual man, should receive an increase. This increase should not be based on this across-the-board concept that because John can turn out x number of gun barrels an hour and Jack can only turn out $\frac{1}{2}x$, both of them should have the same wage increase or both of them should have the same bonus. It is this concept of bargaining in this country that I think has gotten us into the real problem that we are in today. We have dropped, you might say, the initiative, the competitive idea, from our total system of reimbursement to the point that if you and I are working side by side at a lathe, producing exactly the same part and getting the same pay, only my production is rejected by the tune of 10 per cent and yours is rejected by the tune of 1 per cent, are you going to try to improve yourself or am I going to try to improve myself? No. I will say that you are getting $3.00 an hour and that I am getting $3.00 an hour. If you want to work hard enough so that you only have a 1 per cent rejection, that is your business. I am happy having a 10 per cent rejection. But if you should get $3.00 and I should get only $2.50 because I could not produce so well as you, I would be going to night school. I would be working hard to see if I could not improve my proficiency so that I could earn $3.00 an hour. This is one of the factors that I want you to think about as we get into the discussion.

This situation has not come about in this country through normal means. It has come about through abnormal means. We have actually priced ourselves out of the markets in many, many areas of our industry, and we have done it because, I suppose, rightfully zealous labor leaders have taken upon themselves to get more and more and more for their individual members when those individual members did not need it.

So, gentlemen, I think that it is very wise for you to consider this problem because, as you know, in the priesthood you are going to be confronted with both sides of these problems. People are going to come to you either to complain or to object about their treatment, and you are going to have to consider the problem. I think that the Catholic priesthood does so more than any other church, and I do not think that this is wrong. To me, as a conservative, man's problem is not only material; it is equally spiritual. And unless we develop the whole man, we are not developing a man; we are developing a machine that some day will gobble us up by his own lack of spiritual understanding. If there is one thing that leads to these troubles about which we are talking, it is the overbearing desire of people in business, people in unions, people in politics, to present as enticement for man only the material—"what's in it for me"—without stopping to realize that none of us would be here today with the material possessions which we possess if we did not come from stock of strong spiritual base who believed that man has these two sides: spiritual and material. Actually the material side cannot exist without the spiritual side. So you men have a far greater responsibility than we who are in the rather crude business of politics or business, who look at the material side as being an important one. Some of us feel about the spiritual side, but we are not sought after for this kind of advice.

All of these problems about which we are talking relate to man. It is not the fact that we have the nuclear bomb or can fly Mach 3 or sail fifteen hundred feet under the sea. It is what man will do with these things. It is going to take one man to punch that red button. If no man punches that red button, nuclear development can be used for the good of man. If man uses Mach 3 not to carry weapons but to carry people, it can be of value. So it is up to us. The challenge to us is not just wrapped up in what we do about communist Russia, communism generally, but what we do about this thing called human nature. If we in Washington could only pass laws to change human nature, both of us would be out of business and we would have a wonderful world. But so far a new man has not been discovered. The man whom we know is quite a few million years old and for just about as long a time has wandered around with the same human nature which we have. We are selfish; we are kind; we are generous; we hate; we love; we have two sides to every coin that makes up our human nature. It is the same thing with automation. We can beat it. We can conquer it. We will have those who are going to try to make fortunes by throwing people out of work and ignoring them. We will have labor leaders who are going to continue to want unearned wage increases. We will have politicians who try to placate both of them—a solving of their perpetuity on the banks of the

Potomac. It is a disease that infects a man's mind with the idea that if we are not there the country is going to go to hell, in spite of you people. Every time I get to thinking like that, I get out a thick book containing the names of twenty-one hundred senators who preceded me. And we have done all right.

CHAPTER 16

CULTURAL DIMENSIONS
OF THE NEW LEISURE

by REV. W. NORRIS CLARKE, S.J., *Professor of Philosophy, Fordham University*

THE WHOLE BURDEN of this paper is, frankly, to speculate about the future. And I am well aware that such an undertaking needs some defense. Philosophers have frequently been accused of sterile crystal ball gazing, and it might seem that speculation about the future is the type of an idle pastime for intellectuals, particularly the philosophical breed. Possibly in the past this was true to a large extent. I do not think that it is any longer the case. On the contrary, it seems to be now an integral part of the responsibility of all the leaders in any society, in any field, to do just such crystal ball gazing or speculation about the future.

The reason for the new situation is this: a rapid tempo of change has now become one of the characteristic notes of modern society. It is, as we might say in ontological language, a built-in mode of being of our culture. It has been forced upon us partly by technological progress, but also partly by the deliberate planning of industrial society which now systematically stimulates it. All around us today, in all the main fields, there is constant planning for the future and deliberate provoking of change for the future. In business, for example, it is becoming common in the big corporations to set aside a second team of executives whose main job is to plan for the future ten or twenty years. It is too much for one team both to run the enterprise in the present and also to look ahead into the future. Frequently the work of such a second team is not simply to adapt to the future forced upon them, but positively to provoke change, partly for reasons of greater profit, partly for reasons of competitive survival. Businessmen are doing it. So are scientists. The military must obviously do it. Statesmen, educators, leaders in all fields are more and more being forced to do it in order to survive.

Such planning is imperative in a world of constant and rapid change for two reasons: first, because without it you will not be able to cope with the dangers which change suddenly thrusts upon you, and secondly because you will not be able to take advantage of the constructive possibilities of the changes which do occur. It has, therefore, now become an essential part of the responsibilities of leaders in any field systematically to scan and prepare for the future. And I do not mean simply for next year; I mean for ten, twenty, thirty years ahead.

So far, this deliberate planning seems to be going on largely on a piecemeal level—for example, the planning done by special interests, such as corporations, for their own benefit. But who is going to plan ahead for the *humanity* of man? Who is going to plan for his broad overall welfare in the next fifty years? This is certainly beyond the scope of business. Is it the work of sociology? Sociologists are indeed trying to do some of it, but it is perhaps a little too broad even for scientific sociology. Anthropologists, too, are trying their hand at it. But certainly educators, philosophers, and theologians, whose interest should be in the wholeness of man, should begin to shoulder their responsibility for guiding the general movement. Otherwise, we are going to stumble blindly into the future and suddenly find ourselves face to face with some very serious human problems, too late for us to cope adequately with them. History is strewn with the wrecks of civilizations which waited too long to prepare for new challenges.

In order to investigate our present problem realistically, we must start with the facts. The primary fact is that a much larger amount of leisure is in the offing for the masses of our people.

There is, it is true, still some dispute about the fact itself. Some claim that a new trend has appeared, the double job practice. Hence when the working time is cut down, workers will simply take extra jobs and have no more leisure than before. It is quite true that this practice has become at least a short-range trend in certain areas of our economy, both here and in Europe. But in view of the predominantly somber estimates put forward during this week of discussion by experts as to the slow growth of unemployment developing in the wake of automation, it seems fairly certain that in the overall, long-range picture there will have to be a progressive curtailing of the work week in order to maintain full employment in peace time. In the face of growing unemployment, double job holding on a large scale would simply not be socially tolerated. The trend in this direction has been steady over the last hundred years, diminishing from something like an eighty-hour work week in the last century to sixty and then to forty in our own day. Now the predictions are that by the time today's children retire, or within sixty years, the work week will be down to twenty hours. And this is a conservative estimate; some claim a reduction to eight hours a week, but this seems to be more than the crystal ball will yield at present.

What we will then experience for the first time in history is a predominance of leisure over work for the majority of people. Now the first thing which we should notice about this situation is its novelty in human history. As we turn back the pages of time, it is clear that in civilized societies a large amount of leisure has always been the prerogative of the wealthy, the elite, the upper crust of society alone. Work was the lot of the masses; leisure, of the few. Now, for the first time in history, a predominance of leisure over work will become a way of life for the masses and no longer simply for the elite. This in itself is a fact of staggering implications, the more one reflects upon it.

But this is not the only element of novelty in the new situation. What we are faced with is not merely the accession of the masses to a mode of life that will still, as in the past, be enjoyed by the upper level of society. We are faced rather with a paradoxical reversal of the roles of the two groups. If present trends continue, what we shall have is actually less and less leisure for the upper strata of society and more and more leisure for the middle and lower. In order to be successful today, executives in the higher echelons, professional men, scientists, artists, statesmen, generals—in a word, the leaders of our culture—have to work fifty to sixty hours a week regularly if they wish to meet both their responsibilities and their competition. Such people simply cannot get away safely with anything like a forty-hour week. The new leisure, therefore, is really going to be the prerogative principally of the middle and lower levels of society, levels which are also, we must remember, the least educated and humanistically formed—that is to say, the least able to profit constructively from their leisure. As someone put it recently, we shall now have leisure for the masses and work for the classes.

So much for the salient facts which it seems almost certain that we shall have to reckon with. Now let us move into the area of the problems consequent upon these facts. We will not, of course, be able to solve these problems tonight, but my chief hope is to succeed in making you conscious of a radically new set of challenges soon to confront us, and to set you thinking as to what general lines of solution we must begin to plan for.

The most general problem derives from even the most casual reading of history. Wherever in the past there has been a predominance of leisure over work, it has ultimately destroyed every group that has achieved it. Abundant leisure has ordinarily led to absorption in the pursuit of personal pleasure for those possessing it. It seems to be a mysterious, fatal principle of human culture that once a group is freed of the necessity to work, the law of pursuit of personal pleasure begins to take over, becoming its dominant interest. Again and again in the pages of history, this absorption in the pursuit of personal pleasure has led, sooner or later, to degeneration—moral, intellectual, social and finally physical degeneration—and the last stage is the collapse of the society or the emergence of some new ruling class. This is the way in which the cycle runs: wealth, leisure, the pursuit of pleasure, degeneration, collapse or replacement by another group. The record so far has not been a good one for the effects of abundant leisure on those who enjoyed it. What assurance do we have that it will not work the same havoc on us?

And yet the other side of the picture is also true: there has risen an elite with abundant leisure that has frequently stimulated a flowering of the arts, letters and philosophy. Those who possessed the leisure wanted to be entertained and surrounded by beautiful things. So they sponsored artists who, in turn, contributed to the flowering of the various arts.

Among the peoples who passed through such an experience, possibly the Athenians more than any others made the most of their leisure. They were one of the few leisured elites, for example, who developed philosophers on a large scale during such a period. One of the most significant things about the Greek concept and practice of leisure was their distinction between two kinds of leisure: the one, *serious* leisure and the other, what we might call *pastime* leisure. Serious leisure was devoted to such occupations as the theater, the arts, philosophy, politics and athletics. Pastime leisure for them consisted in relaxation, amusement, games (not the same, by the way, as serious athletics)—in a word, anything that provided rest from either work or from serious leisure. Thus we have two kinds of leisure: the one challenging, stimulating and creative, the other relaxing, distracting, restorative.

Yet it must be noted that even in Athens, the plastic artists—architects, painters and sculptors—did not come from this ruling class or elite. They belonged rather to the lower, artisan classes, because to work with the hands was considered below the dignity of the elite. Thus, even the elite of Athens did not produce from among themselves a group of creative artists.

As we ponder these lessons of history, an ominous question mark arises. Will our new leisure be a blessing or a curse? Can the masses of the future survive a predominance of leisure over work, or will the same law of history apply as it has in the past? Such questions are not mere idle speculation. The answers to them may well determine the fate of the whole form of civilization which we see developing around us today.

But since the situation itself will be unique in history, I see no necessity for assuming that the same law must inevitably work again as it has always worked in the past. I am not a partisan of the fatalistic-cyclic view of history.

We are now in a position to narrow down our problem. Which of the two basic ways of spending one's leisure time will predominate when the new leisure comes upon us?

Will it be the unproductive pursuit of personal pleasure and amusement, the Greek pastime leisure, or perhaps more accurately, the Roman—uncreative, self-centered, self-indulgent? Or will it be spent rather in a productive, creative, serious activity that will enrich both the individual and the community?

Here, I believe, is the most crucial and fundamental question facing us. Which is going to predominate: the unproductive rather passive pursuit of pleasure, entertainment and amusement, or productive, enriching, creative activity where the note is one of joy both in self-development as well as in a certain enrichment of the community? If the former predominates, there is no possible doubt that what lies ahead is disaster, the death sentence of our civilization. It has always been so in the past, and it is not too difficult to analyze the intrinsic reasons why it should be so on psychological and moral grounds. The basic principle involved is that where any group of people permits its energies, particularly its mental energies, to lie idle most of the time without the discipline and challenge of hard work, deterioration rapidly sets in, and sooner or later a more vigorous people, a people who are using their energies of mind and body more fully, will challenge their place in the sun and either absorb them or sweep them out of their way.

Absorption in amusement as the main occupation of one's life ends up in the inability to concentrate for very long, to discipline oneself or to stand up under a challenge which demands a long hard pull. People so occupied become incapable of anything but short term activities to meet short term challenges; they simply cannot cope with long range enterprises requiring hard struggle and tenacious endurance. If our masses in the future devote the main part of their leisure time to entertainment, amusement and unproductive activity, we are certainly in for disaster, and will crumble before the rising of the African and Oriental world. A machine whose motor is kept always idling eventually becomes incapable of operating at high speeds.

Now given the inertia and weakness of human nature left to itself, it is quite possible that the masses of our people with their new leisure will tend like a dead weight to the lowest level, towards a vast bread-and-circuses kind of existence, surfeited with entertainment, bored with their gadgets, ever restlessly and purposelessly on the move at higher and higher speeds, and less and less capable of quiet reflection or of any intense, intellectual or spiritual effort. Such is one of the very real possibilities before us if we do not take thought and action now to prepare the children of today for the leisure of tomorrow.

The question of entertainment leads us to digress for a moment on this special problem. One thing certain is that public, professional forms of entertainment and amusement will play a large part in this future leisure. The question then arises: Is it safe to leave the guidance and control of this enormously influential, cultural force exclusively to private enterprise and the play of the market? Many observers feel that government-sponsored TV in other countries has a much better record of quality than our own privately-sponsored system, left as it is to the mercies of the big advertisers. They feel the same way about the record in other countries of government support of the theater and other fine arts. There is too much at stake, they believe, for the cultural health of the nation simply to leave all this to completely unregulated private sources. I am certainly not in the least inclined towards socialism, government interference where private initiative can handle the problem. But urgent problems must be solved. And in practical matters (where no intrinsic moral evil is involved, of course), it is always better to compromise with a theoretical ideal in order to reach some workable solution than to risk total failure by clinging intransigently to an unworkable "best." Besides, there are special aspects to public media of culture which, like education, make it a more appropriate field than business for government intervention. Possibly the best combination might turn out to be a system of basic, private ownership and control strengthened by some degree of government support and control of standards. But we had better not let the matter drift too long. Shrewd political and social observers from abroad who are ordinarily sympathetic to the United States, such as Raymond Aron (at the recent Coring Conference), have been quite frank in expressing their shock and disappointment at the low overall quality of television fare in this country in contrast to that of many other countries and to our own high technical competence.

Let us return now to the central issue we were discussing. We have sketched briefly the darkest possible alternative in our future use of the new leisure. It is time now to take a look at the brighter end of the spectrum of possibilities. This would consist in a predominantly creative, productive, personally and socially enriching utilization of their expanded leisure time by the majority, or at least by a significantly large percentage of the people. If this fork of the road is actually taken, it opens out into truly magnificent and breathtaking perspectives of a massive advance for our culture and potentially for the whole human race toward new levels of basic humanistic development and flowering of the higher faculties of man on a vast, popular scale never attained or even deemed possible before in human history. This may well be the next phase in God's long-range providential plan for the growth of humanity as a whole and of the Mystical Body of Christ, the Church, working as a leaven within it.

I am well aware that this is indeed crystal ball gazing with a vengeance, going beyond what the present lines of evidence permit us to project with any firm probability. I am also aware that many humanists and educators, especially those with a strong classical bent, will look on such a development as naively Utopian and lacking in historical realism on the principle that high humanistic culture by its nature will always be limited to a comparatively small elite and remain out of reach of the masses. And I certainly agree with them that superior culture will always be achieved only by an elite. But higher and lower are nonetheless essentially relative terms, and the fact that the proportionate relations between the number of those on the various levels will always remain roughly the same does not by any means prevent the system as a whole from moving steadily forward and upward. May there not be laws—even humanly controllable laws—of human evolution (cultural as well as physical) just as it seems there are of evolution in the material cosmos leading up to man? Furthermore, since never before in history have the necessary conditions for the possibility of intensive humanistic development existed for the masses in any culture, the negative argument from past history can hardly be considered decisive if the time comes when these conditions for the first time become verified in fact.

Yet, to be hardheadedly realistic, in view of the endemic weakness of human nature and its proneness to yield to the forces of evil at work within it, what we shall most probably be faced with is an unstable, shifting intermingling of both the darker and the brighter possibilities, with the issue up to us (to our vision, courage, initiative, and dedicated, persevering effort, or their opposites) to swing the balance more one way than the other. One of the most crucial and indispensable steps that must be taken in the near future to tip the balance in the right direction is well thought-out education of our children for the leisure to come. And I mean education by the three great institutions equipped for it: the home, the school, and the Church. Since the initiative must ordinarily come from the latter two, however, it is to them that my message is especially addressed.

This leads us naturally to the fundamental, practical, and constructive problem with which the new leisure confronts us, and with which I shall end this paper. What should be the general structure of a program of education for the constructive and enriching use of leisure by civilized man?

The first level, attainable by practically everybody, would seem to me to be the cultivation of some individual manual skill involving the exercise of the individual's special capacities of body, mind, and some degree of esthetic sensitivity, looked on as an expression in matter of each person's individual, human personality. It could be in do-it-yourself repairing, decorating, building around the house, in gardening, in wood or metal working, or in any other of the numberless, useful, manual arts and skills. This might well end up by restoring something like the almost vanished medieval tradition of pride in personal craftsmanship as the expression of one's personality.

Another outlet could be, and I think should be, outdoor life in its two most active and enriching forms: sports or athletics (but as an active participant, not merely a passive spectator), and vital contact with and exploration of the world of nature, especially living nature. Already the massive boom in activities like pleasure boating and outdoor camping indicates a sound instinct in our people seeking self-expression. Analogous to this, though on a higher cultural level, could be classed travel, especially to learn of other peoples and cultures or our own past. In the long run, this can gradually and unobtrusively knit the bonds of human brotherhood and solidarity more closely together (not to mention building up the visible unity of the Mystical Body on earth), and also consolidate more firmly man's conscious possession and domination of the globe that has been given him by God as the arena of his self-development by work and play. Needless to add, the imminent possibilities of space travel open up almost limitless new horizons on this level.

The next level would be that of continued self-education through reading, education, or TV, by which everyone could make an effort to assimilate as much as he was able and willing of the accumulated wisdom and culture, scientific, literary, artistic, religious, etc., of mankind. Consider the possibilities if something like this could be made a part of our cultural ethos as taken for granted, as expected of every up-to-date citizen, as simply "the thing to do," like having a car or being able to write. Conversation might even return as a fine art again, this time as a popular art (now I am really dreaming!).

The next level would lead us into the fine arts, and by this I do not mean merely appreciation but also creative participation. Already there are some three million amateur painters in the country, and admissions to serious concerts of music have gone up 60 per cent in ten years. It is a matter of considerable dispute just how widely distributed is the ability of creative self-expression through the fine arts. There is no way of knowing for sure until the opportunity to realize their potentialities is made available to the masses. It does seem reasonably certain, however, that some significant talent along these lines is far more widely shared than has so far had the chance to manifest itself. Even though the number always remained a minority, it would not seem at all improbable that widespread opportunity and encouragement for "ordinary" people to try their hand in some way at painting, sculpture, or any one of the various fine arts, old and new, might well prove the stimulus to the greatest flowering of art in history, the principle being that the broader the base, the higher the pyramid will reach. At least the minimum that might realistically be expected is a continual movement from the higher levels of the useful arts and good craftsmanship toward the lower levels of the fine arts, if indeed it is possible to separate the two in any watertight way. Who can say for certain that the reason why there has never been any mass movement in art before is not largely lack of opportunity, lack of systematic education both in the appreciation and practice of the arts, and lack of widespread social esteem and approval for the serious cultivation of such talents? Already for some years observers have noted the remarkable renaissance of interest in and teaching of art in schools and colleges around the country. There are even signs that our own Jesuit schools are at last waking up to the role of the fine arts in the full development of the educated man, after several hundred years of almost exclusive concentration on literature, as though she had no sisters among the Muses.

The last outlet—and we have space only to mention it— would be on the level of greater personal participation in the civic and other public life of the community, something which most people simply do not have the time to enter into at present.

This brings up the important question, which we can only call to your attention here, of whether the use of leisure should be primarily individual or primarily social. It may be that for a while at least, as long as the conditions of work tend to depersonalize the individual and submerge him as an anonymous unit in the mass, as is true for so many today, the principal function of leisure will be to restore the balance and give an opportunity for the individual initiative, self-assertion, and self-expression that has little or no outlet during the time of work. His leisure will enable a man to rediscover himself as a person. Yet we are also learning more and more that social or group activity on a truly personal basis is not a stifler but a marvelous developer and releaser of authentic, personal individuality. No one is fully an "I" save in conscious relation to some "Thou." There can be no authentic "We" save through the free, personal coming together of authentic "I's."

Secondly, start planning now how to introduce into our educational program some kind of systematic orientation of our students toward preparing for the fruitful and creative use of their future leisure. What profound repercussions it would have on our future culture if every student were made to feel it is an integral part of the educated man's training for life, part of his responsibility to himself, to his family and to his community, to prepare himself for the fruitful use of the leisure which he will have as an adult! We stumbled blindly and thoughtlessly into the industrial age and are still trying to heal many of the wounds that resulted. The atomic age burst so suddenly upon us that we had no time to prepare for it and are just beginning to be aware of the magnitude of its problems. The automation revolution is being ushered in under much better control. But one of its most far-reaching aftermaths will be what some have called "the leisure revolution." If, as I together with many others believe, the new leisure will either make or break the civilization of our grandchildren or great-grandchildren, then surely we owe it both to them and to God, our common Father, to prepare in time for this new spiritual challenge to human survival and growth whose coming portents are written too clearly in the sky for us to have any excuse for not seeing them.

CHAPTER 17

POLITICAL, SOCIAL, AND ECONOMIC IMPLICATIONS OF AUTOMATION

by Eugene J. McCarthy, *U. S. Senator*
(D) from Minnesota

THE QUESTION OF automation is one which has received a great deal of attention within recent years. It has given the sociologists new terms over which to be concerned; it has given the economists new titles, at least, for articles in popular journals; it has given the politicians subject matter for insertions in the *Congressional Record;* and it has created very special problems for the working people of America and for all those who are concerned about their welfare and about the general welfare of this country.

The optimistic view is that automation is the fulfillment of the promise: that it will carry humanity into the upland pastures where the sun shines all the time and all of man's material needs be well supplied.

The extreme pessimistic view, on the other hand, sees automation as heralding the end of humanity or at least the end of any useful function or work on the part of mankind. It sees the need for human effort declining in a kind of geometric retrogression.

The theoretical economists are inclined to take an

213

optimistic view of automation and of its potential effects. Most of them, of course, assert that automation will increase production. Peter Drucker, writing in *Harper's Magazine,* April 1955, states his opinion that automation will prevent the extremes of "boom" and "bust" since it requires the investment of large amounts of capital expenditure independent of cyclical changes in the economy. In the same article, he expressed the opinion that automation would promote stability in employment since with automation labor would more and more be in the nature of a capital resource and wages would assume the character of fixed costs. This point of view stated in 1955 was similar to one expressed by Professor Slichter some twenty-five years earlier and cited by Professor Clyde E. Dankert of Dartmouth College in an article on automation and employment prepared for the Special Committee on Unemployment Problems of the United States Senate in 1959. The Slichter viewpoint was that because of the high overhead costs which continue while expensive machines are idle and because of other factors, "it seems likely that within a generation unemployment will become a problem of secondary importance."

The experience of the last thirty years, and even more pertinently the experience of the last five years, do not prove conclusively the soundness of these speculative opinions of Professor Drucker and Professor Slichter. Whatever the combination of causes may be, the fact is that there has been serious unemployment in the United States in the years since World War II. The rate today is nearly 7 per cent, and the number of unemployed has been running at about 5,500,000 persons. Of this number approximately 900,000 have been out of work for more than 6 months.

Both in terms of absolute numbers and also as a percentage of the working force, unemployment has been

214

increasing since the end of World War II. There have been three identifiable recessions. In the recovery that followed each of these recessions, there has not been a comparable recovery in employment. The rate of unemployment at the peak of each of the last three prosperity periods has been higher than that which existed in the previous one. Unemployment at the peak of the prosperity of 1953 was 3 per cent; at the peak of the prosperity of 1956 it was 3.9 per cent; at the peak of the prosperity of 1959 it was 4.8 per cent; and today when production figures are making new records, unemployment is running at just short of 7 per cent.

Trends are evident, too if one looks at specific industries or areas of the economy. Employment in agriculture has been greatly affected by both technical and nontechnological change. In 1860 workers in agriculture made up about 60 per cent of the civilian labor force; in 1960 such workers make up less than 10 per cent. There has been a definite decline not only in the relative number of persons engaged in agriculture, but a decline in absolute numbers as well. In recent years there has been a significant shift out of agricultural employment and with the improvements that have been and are being made in agricultural technology and methods, unemployment and under-employment among agricultural workers can be expected to increase. Further advances in this field will eliminate more workers including a large percentage of the two million migrant workers. "Return of the masses to their normal and healthful existence as tillers of the soil," proposed in 1870 as a solution to unemployment in the cities, cannot be proposed today.

Employment in manufacturing relative to the size of our population has shown little change over the years. While the civilian population of the country increased by 61.7 per cent between 1919 and 1956, employment in manufacturing industries increased by 60.5 per cent. In absolute numbers, employment in manufacturing has increased much more slowly than has employment of nonproduction salaried workers. Between 1950 and 1956, for example, the number of employees in manufacturing increased by 7.1 per cent while those in nonproduction categories grew by 40 per cent. Technological changes in manufacturing have been so extensive and so rapid that the increase in manufacturing employment has not quite kept up with the increase in population.

In the electrical industry, according to testimony of James B. Carey, president of the International Association of Electrical and Machine Workers, employment of production workers dropped from 925,000 in 1953 to 836,000 in February, 1961, despite a large increase in the production of electrical appliances. According to Carey, also, instrument production, which has been expanding in recent years, now employs 30,000 fewer production workers than it did 7 years ago—a drop of some 15 per cent. In the manufacture of refrigerators and washing machines, the job decrease has been about 18 per cent.

The testimony of Patrick E. Gorman, secretary-treasurer of the Amalgamated Meatcutters and Butcher Workers of North America, pointed out that although meat production was up a percentage point in 1960 to 26,900,000,000 pounds, the total number of workers went down from 191,000 to 161,000. Despite increasing production, employment in this industry between 1956 and 1960 has been decreasing at a rate of more than 7,000 a year.

According to the testimony of David McDonald, president of the United Steelworkers of America, the year 1960 was almost identical with the year 1950 in terms of steel production and shipments. Yet in the year 1960, production-worker employment in steel averaged 461,800 compared with 540,000 in 1950—a decline of almost 80,000.

In the bituminous coal mining industry, the number of workers declined from 344,000 in 1950 to 211,000 in 1956; and in the anthracite industry from 71,000 to 27,000 in the same period, while railroad employment was declining from 1,391,000 to 1,191,000.

In the clerical field automation has taken over the work of many clerks, but because of the increase in paper work, the number of people employed, even with machines, has tended to increase.

In the retail trade there have been some changes: introduction of vending machines has replaced a number of clerks as is indicated by the volume of business done by automatic machines which in 1960 totalled some $4,000,000,000.

Any moral judgment concerning automation should take into account really two things: first, the nature of work and the effect of automation upon man as a worker; and secondly, the consequences in terms of social and economic and cultural change that may result from automation. If work in itself were a curse, then a fully automated productive system would be wholly desirable—a kind of temporal redemption. On the other hand, if work is considered as a temporal punishment, elimination of labor would be a most dangerous venture.

There are those who say that with automation there will be demands for greater skill and greater intellectual response and that this work will be truly more creative and that much drudgery will be eliminated. There are those on the other hand who say "no," that work will become increasingly uncreative and that whereas this work may not be drudgery according to the traditional or classical definition usually applied to manual work, there will

217

be a kind of intellectual drudgery having a depressing effect upon the mind, discouraging, if not eliminating the need for, the exercise of creative talents and creative capacity.

Work is an activity which for most men is an expression of the intellectual virtue of art. It should be, as Pope John has stressed in a recent encyclical, "an expression of the human person." If it is established that automation dehumanizes the worker, then we must pass a moral judgment upon it since work which is becoming to man should allow the use of intelligence and the exercise of moral responsibility and of creative talent.

It is not yet clear as to just what the effects of automation will be. There are those who say that with the advance of automation there will be a need for more advanced technicians, more supervisors, more managers, that we will need more people and a higher percentage of the working force who are better trained and better skilled as technicians, as engineers, and the like. There are those, on the other hand, who say that this result will not necessarily follow and that, in fact, fewer skilled people will be needed; that workers will not have to have the same degree of mastery of technique and of knowledge that they now do need; that many will be displaced or demoted from semi-skilled and semi-professional positions which they hold at the present time to positions requiring less skill and less intelligence and more limited application. There are some who say that the effect of today's automation is different from the effect of early mechanization and the application of power and the development of the factory system because in earlier times when people were displaced, they could move down to take jobs which required somewhat less skill or they might move up to more skilled positions. But that today there is little room at the top and little room at the bottom since automation is removing even those jobs which required the least in the way of skill. If this is the case and if unemployment consequently is to become a permanent problem and possibly become an even more serious problem, the moral responsibility of society to attempt to ease and to overcome these effects is, I think, clear. If automation is to eliminate jobs at the middle, then certainly we must undertake to make more room at the top by training more people for professions, more skilled occupations and at least make enough room at the bottom so that people can earn a living with some decency and some certainty.

There are some who say that with automation there will be more jobs for women, and some who say that with automation there will be fewer jobs for women. There are those experts who say that because of the greater investment in capital, the practice of employing swing shifts, if not night shifts as well, will increase. If the practice of running factories twenty-four hours a day does increase, if it becomes a widespread practice, this development certainly will have significant implications with regard to family life, with regard to the whole structure of society.

Without trying to form a final judgment as to how bad things will become as automation progresses or how good they will be, one can fairly assume that there will be problems in the future, some of which, at least in part, will be caused by automation. Accepting that there will be problems, we must raise two questions: one, the question as to whether anything can be done; and second, assuming that something can and should be done, the question of how it should be done and of by whom it should be done.

Since automation touches upon the industrial and business world, immediate responsibility rests upon those who are most directly involved: those who are responsible for the leadership of organized labor, as well as unorganized labor, share the burden of responsibility with management and the directors of industry. Beyond these, of course, everyone who in any way participates either as a producer or a consumer in our economy must accept some measure of responsiblity. The responsibility of these is most likely to be expressed through some form of governmental activity.

Long before the nineteenth century when the problems of mechanization and of the factory system became matters of general concern, Queen Elizabeth denied a patent for a knitting machine sought by one Mr. William Lee because, as she is quoted as having said, "I have too much regard for my people who obtain their bread by knitting." In the middle of the nineteenth century Karl Marx made his recommendations as to what the response of government should be. He was not alone. John Stuart Mill, writing about the same time as a philosopher of liberal economics, said that there cannot be a more "legitimate object of the legislator's care than the interests of those who are thus sacrificed to the gain of their fellow citizens and posterity—those displaced by changing methods of production." Pope John XXIII in his encyclical *Mater et Magistra,* acknowledges and clarifies this community and governmental responsibility.

How then do we proceed? There are those who say that what needs to be done and what government should do —what everyone should do—is to stimulate general economic growth so that those workers who are now in surplus will be reabsorbed and through increased productivity, the general needs, the needs of all the people, will be more effectively and more fully met. Certainly with automation there is potential for increased production. To the extent that the machine merely replaces man and that other pressure points in the economy are not relieved, there is no absolute certainty that with automation there

220

will be increased production. Some of the labor spokesmen have raised this point, saying that increased hourly
output without increase in total production and without
a growing market is, in their words, merely a formula for
economic distress to be followed or accompanied by social
and political disturbance.

In some industries attempts have been made to work
out the adjustments that result from automation or increased productivity or displacement of men by machines.
In the case of the coal mining industry and the United
Mine Workers under John L. Lewis, special funds were
established to help to relieve distress and the pressure of
transition in a period of automation, increased use of other
fuels and changes in user practices. In the railroad industry a similar practice is followed and attempts are made
to make adjustments toward a reduced labor force by ac-
cretion, that is, not rehiring to replace men who retire
or leave the employment of the company for some other
reason.

On a broader scale improved unemployment compensation programs, supported out of general revenue or by employers, have been proposed, and, in one proposal, supported by a special tax to be placed upon machines. As a
machine displaced a man and became more productive, a
portion of the increased productivity would be drawn off
in the way of taxes. This tax in turn would be used to
establish a fund which would meet the special problems
of readjustment or of existence of the displaced worker.

None of these approaches, of course, meets the problem
of providing employment for young people or new people
who come into the working force or for those who may
wish to change from one type of employment to another.
Proposals have been made for a shorter working day or for
a shorter working week or for a shorter working year or
for a shorter working lifetime—earlier retirement, longer

vacations. All of these, of course, are deserving of some consideration and are receiving some. A program of retraining has been advocated and has received approval in the Congress. There is, of course, a need for retraining, but the possibility of its solving the total problem is extremely remote. The distressed area redevelopment legislation that has been approved is basically distressed industry legislation. Proposals have been made and provisions have been made for a geographical shift to try to help the surplus working force to move from one area of the country to another where job opportunities are greater. Proposals in this field have been somewhat limited. They have been subject to negotiations by labor unions. It has been suggested that tax-deduction, at least, be given for the costs incurred by a worker in moving himself and his family from one part of the country to another in order to obtain work.

Each of these proposals has in it some potentiality for good. Some of them can be made effective through government action; most of them, certainly, can be assisted by government. Others can either be advanced primarily by negotiation between labor and management or by unilateral action on the part of management and some measure of public response.

It is important that this whole problem be considered in a somewhat broader context of ideas. One challenge to capitalism and the free enterprise system posed by the Marxists is that whereas the capitalistic system is able to produce in great quantities, it does not have within itself the potential for working out the problems of distribution of its produce. This, I think, in part is a proper analysis because certainly the problem of distribution is a complicated one and a difficult one. I am inclined to think that the more serious problem developing now is not that of the distribution of production, but rather the problem of the distribution of participation in productive effort and productive work. This is of more fundamental and really primary consideration. We have been challenged to work out devices and procedures under which every person can have a part and a claim and a share in the productive effort of our economy, and on the basis of that participation, a claim to a share of that which is produced. This raises some practical questions as to how we shall procure this participation. We are moving, I believe, toward a point where a difficult choice may have to be made. The point has not yet been reached, but there are trends or signs of development which are significant. The choice, in rather broad terms, is between a kind of corporate feudalism and a more national economic and social structure.

Through the years, many of the larger corporations have developed a structure in which, through various devices, the employees increasingly are tied to the company: pension programs, medical and health insurance, special unemployment compensation, supplemental unemployment benefits, profit sharing, job rights, and a number of other benefits, either real or prospective, create bonds between the employee and the company for which he works. Many of these programs have been sought by organized labor.

A rather extreme manifestation of this was reflected in a *Fortune* magazine series four or five years ago entitled "The Wives of Management," in which the concern of the corporation not only over the life of its employee while on the job, but concern over the social structure of which he was a part was expressed. It was suggested by one corporate director that really the corporation should not wait until after the marriage, but ought to be concerned about giving some direction and some guidance to its employees in the selection of wives. Possibilities of this kind of direct and indirect control are practically unlimited, especially now that calculators and computers and mechanical brains have been perfected to do the sorting.

The choice may be to fix more and more responsibility upon corporations to accept that their employees are their charges and to insist that the employees receive in return for their work a fair share from the production which results from the operation of the particular industry, and this share could be defined so as to include not only immediate wages, but all those things which are now commonly lumped under the title of "fringe benefits."

On the other hand the decision may be to establish or maintain national programs of security: to improve the social security program so as to make it more effective, to have a national program of health insurance, to have a more satisfactory unemployment compensation program based upon national standards. The decision need not be absolute on the one side or on the other, but certainly there is a need for consideration of the possibility that the corporate plans may very well have the attempt of limiting the economic and social mobility as well as the general freedom of individual employees and that this individual freedom may be somewhat secured by national programs which do establish a reasonable base, leaving to the individual a measure of freedom and a greater measure of choice. This problem exists not only for the working man but for professional and for semi-professional people.

An improved, reasonable, adequate national retirement program would make it easier for an employee who wanted to leave a particular job or put him in a position at least where when he wanted to leave, he would not be forced to stay on saying, "I cannot leave because of my pension program," but he could make the choice of leaving and carrying with him some measure of security against old age. Or if there was a national program of health insurance, a person who might wish to leave would not be held in his original job because he could not afford to give up his medical insurance program. Or if a reasonably effective national unemployment compensation program were in effect, a person who wished to leave the employ of one company or one industry to go on to another would not be bound to stay with the first one because if he were to leave he would lose all the benefits and rights that he had accumulated in that original job.

Along with these problems, I think, is a need that we give some thought to the basic concept of ownership in our society and in our economy. It is generally recognized now that to most people in the United States ownership today does not mean what it did one hundred years ago. Generally the great body of ownership is not in tangible, identifiable real property but exists in claims to income. This is certainly true in the case of the corporate stockholder and of those who hold bonds, insurance policies, and so forth. Most workers do not own the tools with which they work, but lay claim to a job and to a salary or wages which they are to receive for performing their work. The question of ownership is involved not in the absolute sense but in a relative sense in such issues as that of the closed shop or the right of a person to hold a job.

In a hearing before the Congress several years ago, this point was rather clearly made by a comparison of argument being made before two separate committees. One a Committee of the Interior, which was proposing to change the lease arrangements on public lands which were being used for cattle grazing. The request was for a change in the terms of the leases so as to give the individuals holding the leases modified and greatly strengthened rights to use and of transfer. A witness in favor of the legislation supported the proposition with two arguments: first, that those who already held the leases should be given the new leases because of "priority," that is, because they were already there; and secondly, because of "stability," since the witness argued that to put the leases up to auction might have the effect of disturbing the whole community. At the same time, in hearings which were being held before the Labor Committee on the question of the closed shop, spokesmen for the same group that argued for property rights based upon priority and stability opposed the closed shop while the spokesmen for organized labor argued that the worker's right to the job should be recognized for two reasons: first, "priority," because the worker was already there; and secondly, for reasons of "stability" of society. In each case the traditional or original, sometimes called natural, claims to ownership—occupancy, priority, and stability—were recognized.

There have been two rather significant federal court decisions touching upon the vested rights of employees. When Gemmer, a Detroit unit of the Ross Gear and Tool Manufacturing Company of Indiana, decided to move to Lebanon, Tennessee, and declined to offer transfers to the main body of its United Auto Workers employees, a bargaining committee of the Auto Workers sued on behalf of the employees. This year Judge Kaess sustained a contention holding that the rights claimed by the employees extend "beyond the time limitations of the collective bargaining agreement." They apply to the company plant "regardless of physical location under this and previous contracts" and that the company "has an obligation and duty to rehire on the basis of seniority" employees laid off in Detroit even though the move to Lebanon may terminate the role of their union as their bargaining agent. This rule expanded an earlier decision of the Second Circuit Court of Appeals in the case known as the Glidden case, in which in 1957 the Second Circuit held that employees had acquired by their continuous service "vested rights" that the company could not unilaterally deny.

The development of automation intensifies problems which originally developed with the increased use of power, by mechanization, and by the factory system. These problems must be solved within a moral framework. What is called for is the application of reason—the assertion of the power of reason to exert some control over life and give it at least a better direction.

The effect of automation on man, the worker, is not yet clear, but as a principle of judgment, we cannot accept that what happens as a result of automation can or should be left, in the language of Pope John, to the "mechanical play of market forces . . . but it should be determined by justice and equity."

CHAPTER 18

THE ETHICAL AFTERMATH OF AUTOMATION

by RT. REV. MSGR. GEORGE G. HIGGINS,
Director, Social Action Department,
National Catholic Welfare Conference

MY EMBARRASSMENT IN POSING as an expert on the moral implications of automation is to some extent relieved or diminished by the fact that, to the best of my knowledge, hardly anybody else in this country can properly claim to be an eminent authority in this particular field of social ethics. I was made painfully—or, from a more selfish point of view, consolingly—aware of this fact when I started to do my homework for the preparation of this paper. I discovered that American theologians and moral philosophers have published very little of a scholarly or scientific nature on the ethical or moral aspects of automation. The reason for this is rather obvious, and, to my way of thinking, it reflects more credit than blame on the theologians and moral philosophers. The reason is that automation, in the specialized sense in which the word is being used at this Seminar, is not only a relatively new phenomenon but one which, because of its technical complexity, initially baffles, if it does not actually frighten the average layman, including the average theologian and moral philosopher.

A scholarly or scientific theology of automation cannot be developed in the vacuum of a seminary or university library. Neither, of course, can it be developed in the vacuum of a scientific laboratory or technical workshop, much less in the antiseptic vacuum of an automized factory. This is merely another way of saying that an adequate theology of automation cannot be developed without the closest and most intimate kind of collaboration between the theologian, the scientist, and the practical technician, with all of them learning from as well as teaching one another in the best tradition of intellectual cooperation. In this list of collaborators I should also have included the labor leader and the businessman, as well as the economist, the sociologist, and the political scientist, all of whom have a legitimate interest in automation and are capable of contributing to the solution of the complex problems which automation will almost inevitably bring in its wake.

In this connection, may I say that this particular conference is a significant step in the right direction. This is not a gathering of scientists and technicians consulting with one another in a vacuum. To a certain extent at least, it is a diversified gathering of specialists from several different disciplines studying a problem which, at least in its implications for society, is too big and too difficult for any single, isolated group of specialists to cope with effectively. I sincerely congratulate the members of the program committee, therefore, on the breadth of their vision in scheduling a discussion of the economic, social, and moral aspects of automation instead of limiting the program exclusively to the purely scientific and technical aspects of the subject. We shall all come away from the conference with a deeper and more rounded understanding of the subject for having had the opportunity—which is all too rare in our highly specialized society—to exchange information and points of view with competent and experienced men from several different but related disciplines, professions, or occupations.

This has been an unconscionably long and, to some of you perhaps, a rather irrelevant introduction to what should be and will be, I promise you, a relatively brief discussion of some of the moral aspects of automation and its impact on society. There was, however, a certain conscious and deliberate method to my madness in stressing so emphatically at the outset the complexity of the problem before us. I wanted to warn against the danger involved in jumping to facile or oversimplified conclusions about automation and its impact on society.

Keeping that danger in mind, let us consider a few of the more obvious problems which would immediately suggest themselves, I think, to any theologian or moral philosopher —or, for that matter, to any well-informed member of the general public—if he were called upon to discuss the subject assigned to me this evening. Solutions to some of these problems will be mentioned, in passing, but in view of the limited time at our disposal they will not—indeed, they cannot—be adequately discussed.

I should add, by way of a further parenthesis or introductory note, that my partial listing of problems and solutions will be borrowed either literally or in paraphrase from three significant and fairly detailed statements on automation made by Pope Pius XII. These three documents show a more profound grasp of the spiritual and moral implications of automation than anything else I have read on the subject. They do not constitute a complete textbook on the moral theology of automation, but they do provide an extremely useful outline for such a treatise.

The first question that suggests itself with regard to automation can be stated as follows: Is automation in itself a blessing or a curse from the point of view of theology or moral philosophy? The answer, of course, is neither. Or, to put the answer in more positive terms, automation can be either a blessing or a curse, depending on the way it is used and the ends or purposes for which it is used by human beings, who are created a little less than the angels and, sputnik to the contrary, are still the appointed stewards of the universe, privileged to cooperate with its Creator in its further development and subject to His immutable laws of right and wrong.

Pope Pius XII, in one of the documents already alluded to, summarizes this two-pronged, yes-and-no Christian reaction to automation as follows: The development of automation, he says, "should be considered with prudence and healthy optimism." "If the machine," he continues, "which only yesterday was still a gradually improving and stronger tool in the service of man, can henceforth replace the hand which grasps and guides, the eye which observes and controls and even, for certain definite purposes, the consciousness which watches and the memory which preserves an always available past—if the machine is substituted not only for the worker himself, but also for the bookkeeper and to a certain extent for the technician, thus opening to industry unsuspected possibilities—for all this we should only give thanks to God who has enabled man to accomplish such works."

So much for the positive or optimistic aspect of the Christian reaction to automation. But, His Holiness continues in a more negative tone, it is up to Christians, who "know the greatness of man in the eyes of God," to remind the world of the fundamental truth that technological progress is not an end in itself and that it does not find within itself "the principle of its own regulation."

We could profitably spend several hours prayerfully mediating on this very basic and very simple truth, but time will permit us to mention only a few of its implications. Automation, as we have indicated, is not an end in itself. It is a means—a potentially blessed and beneficent means—to promote the welfare of human beings, their spiritual and cultural as well as their material welfare. Negatively this means, on the face of it, that automation would prove to be a curse rather than a blessing to humanity if it were to be used selfishly to increase the profits of a few at the expense of the many or, more specifically, if it were to be introduced so rapidly or so haphazardly as to result in unemployment or even in underemployment in a given region or country.

"In this matter," as Pope Pius XII has stated, "we cannot adopt the false maxim which in the past led some politicians to sacrifice an entire generation for the benefits expected to accrue to following ones." Or again, as His Holiness stated in an earlier document: "A totalitarian economy can assure the future by destroying the present generation. A Christian, although he can ask for sacrifice, does not have the right to sacrifice his brother."

This whole question as to whether or not automation will lead to unemployment or severe underemployment is understandably charged with a great deal of emotion. Nevertheless I have been pleased to note in attending other conferences of this type that increasingly, as time goes on, it seems to be possible for labor and management to discuss the question realistically and with their feet firmly planted on the ground. I might add, parenthetically, that scientists and technicians who have had no experience or training in the socio-economic field would be well advised to stay out of the argument or at least to recognize the limits of their professional competence. I say this rather bluntly because I have heard engineers and technicians at previous conferences on automation talk palpable nonsense about the so-called laws of economics—as though

233

these laws operated as automatically or inevitably as the laws of physics and the other natural sciences which are the specialty of the technicians. Forgive me for this rather discourteous parenthesis, which was intended merely to add to the sport of our discussion later on.

Coming back to labor and management and their joint responsibility—in cooperation with the government—to make automation serve the general economic and social welfare, let me refer again to the several statements of Pope Pius XII on this subject. In all of these documents great stress is laid on the importance of labor-management cooperation for the protection of the rights and the interests of workers affected by automation.

"Recent instances show," His Holiness states, for example, "that the risk of mass unemployment as a result of the sudden modernization of factories is not illusory." A "judicious participation of workers in the effort of expansion," he continues, would not only help to avoid this danger but would also "bring about a progressive and profound transformation of the present condition of the working class."

His Holiness makes substantially the same point in a more recent statement. "The present problem," he says, " . . . is to harmonize to a greater degree the interests of management and labor, and to make them aware of their common destiny in the social economy . . ." His advice to labor and management is extremely simple: "it is better to bargain than to fight." This, he says, "is the only word which both . . . can make their own in the light of their own conscience and before the world."

It is gratifying to note that within recent months two prominent Americans—a consulting engineer and a nationally known labor leader—have issued statements which closely parallel the Vatican's thinking on this important subject.

James J. Lamb, former executive staff consultant of the

234

Remington Rand Division of the Sperry Rand Corporation, presented his views on the social and economic effects of automation in two lectures at Catholic University's Summer Institute of Catholic Social Action. Though job dislocation resulting from automation is on a minor scale at the present time, he said, nevertheless it is of "painful concern" to the semi-skilled workers immediately affected. To meet this problem, he continued, a suitable plan for the retraining of these workers should be put into effect in adequate time. It is even more important, Mr. Lamb said, that adequate provision be made for the retraining of older industrial employees whose skill is entirely manual. "It is this group," he emphasized, "that requires the best cooperative effort of employers, workers' organizations, vocational educators, and of the worker himself for its solution. Passing the buck from one to the other will not accomplish the necessary social purpose."

Mr. Lamb's deep concern as an engineer with the social and economic effects of automation is refreshing, and frankly, rather surprising. It has been our impression heretofore that the engineering profession, by and large, is not so articulate as it ought to be on matters of social justice.

It is less surprising but equally gratifying to find that George Harrison—the highly respected president of the Brotherhood of Railway Clerks—has also insisted on the importance of labor-management cooperation as the only just and sensible method of planning the changeover to automation in the railroad industry.

Mr. Harrison is not opposed to the introduction of automation in the railroad industry, but he strongly urges that the workers adversly affected be treated fairly. Wherever possible, he says, workers should be adequately trained to operate the new equipment and then be paid in accordance with their newly acquired skills.

Those workers who are permanently dislocated by the

introduction of automation, Mr. Harrison maintains, "are entitled to reasonable consideration on such matters as severance pay and supplemental unemployment benefits, reimbursement for any loss on the sale of homes or obligations under leases, expenses occasioned by transfer of residence to another city, and the continuation of coverage of employees and their dependents under the health and welfare agreements." All of these matters, he says, must be subject to collective bargaining, preferably in the form of a national agreement which would set down the procedure and terms for the protection of employees affected by automation.

Thank God for the likes of Mr. Lamb and Mr. Harrison. May their tribe increase! Given enough engineers, labor leaders, and employers with such intelligent concern for human values, there is every reason to anticipate that automation will redound to the greater glory of God and to the welfare of the human race.

There is every reason to believe, incidentally, that Mr. Harrison's constructive approach to automation is the dominant point of view in labor circles. That is to say, the majority of labor leaders not only in this country but also in the other industrialized countries of the world are prepared to welcome automation so long as it serves the general economic welfare. For an excellent summary of labor's attitude with regard to automation I refer you to an article entitled "The Trade Union Movement Faces Automation" by Alfred Braunthal, Head of the Economic and Social Department of the International Confederation of Free Trade Unions. Mr. Braunthal's article is published in the December 1957 issue of *International Labour Review*, official monthly publication of the International Labor Organization in Geneva, Switzerland.

Up to this point, we have been talking about a limited type of labor-management cooperation aimed specifically at

236

solving the particular problem created either directly or indirectly by the development and introduction of automation—e.g., the problem of displacement of workers and the even more difficult problem of adjusting wages and hours to meet the changing conditions of changing times. Labor-management cooperation in the solution of limited problems of this type is a step in the right direction, but hardly more than that. In other words, labor-management cooperation is needed not only for the solution of the specific problems created by automation but also for the development of an overall policy of economic and social stability and prosperity. This is merely another way of saying that the solution to the economic and social problems created by automation depends in large measure on the general health of our economic system.

There are some, of course, who think that economic planning should be carried on exclusively, or almost exclusively, by the government. Obviously, as Pope Pius XII points out in one of his above-mentioned statements on automation, more government planning will be needed, at least in certain countries, to meet the enormously complicated economic and social problems which are likely to confront us in the emerging era of automation. But this planning, he warns, "need not and cannot be identical with more or less absolute state control. It cannot because the independence of families and the freedom of citizens are by nature linked with the sound functioning of private property as an order-producing institution."

This problem of striking the proper balance in the political order between the individual and society—so perfectly exemplified in the Church by the "fellowship of all in relation to all"—has never been perfectly resolved at any stage in human history or in any given country, including our own. The pendulum of history has swung back and forth between the extremes of individualism and collectivism in one form or another. At the present time, taking the human race as a whole, the scales would seem to be weighted in favor of collectivism. This is not true, of course, in the United States, which, in spite of all its faults, is one of the most successful political experiments in the history of the world. We have probably come as close as any people in history to striking a happy balance between the extremes of individualism and collectivism, but we dare not rest on our laurels. We have yet to formulate a completely satisfactory theory of democracy. Even today, as one political theorist has recently pointed out, we still concentrate too single-mindedly upon the individual as the sole unit of society and upon the State as the sole source of legitimate power. To be sure, we do not officially prohibit the formation of voluntary associations midway between the isolated individual and the State. On the contrary, we have an abundance of such organizations—many more, indeed, than one would suspect from reading our official mythology. Nevertheless we have not yet formulated a theory of democracy that includes these organizations, that makes them indispensable to free, representative government.

No other country in the world is better prepared than our own to direct this quest for community in the right direction. And no other country is under a greater obligation to do so. To cite an example which is of particular interest to me because of my work at NCWC, it can be said, without fear of contradiction, that never before in modern times has a country so important as the United States been in such a favorable position to combine the values of prudent and sound economic planning with the values of freedom under a system of private enterprise. In many other parts of the world it has been too readily taken for granted that economic planning for the general welfare is primarily the responsibility of government and only secondarily, if at all, the responsibility of free associations of workers and employers. This has led to various types and varying degrees of station, some less objectionable than others, but none of them desirable, to say the least, from the point of view of Christian social teaching. If we in the United States can succeed in ushering in a new era of labor-management-government cooperation which will combine the values of planning with the values of freedom, we will have the satisfaction of knowing that by our example of Christian brotherhood in action we will have benefited the rest of the world as well as our own country.

Let me emphasize, in conclusion, that it would be a serious mistake to imagine that all of the moral and spiritual problems connected with automation are in the socio-economic order. On the contrary, automation is likely to have its greatest impact, either for weal or for woe, in the broad field of culture, including education and religion. Surely one of its inevitable by-products will be an increase in leisure for the masses of our people. We haven't the time, even if we had the competence, to discuss this problem in detail. But this much can be said with certainty —that leisure as such, like automation as such, is not necessarily either a blessing or a curse, It all depends on what people do with it, or as Pope Pius XII stated, "Man has leisure not only as a natural and proper relief, but to improve his faculties, to better fulfill his religious, family, and social duties, and to make himself physically and spiritually better fit for work." Thus the importance of deepening and strengthening our cultural and religious values, in the absence of which automation will tend to make automatons out of men, who are created in the image and likeness of God.

This presents a challenge not only to our churches and our schools but to the mass media of communication and entertainment and indeed to every other cultural agency in our complex society. Obviously, however, it presents a very immediate and particularly compelling challenge to our schools, both public and private, at every level of education. Since the lanching of sputnik just a few short years ago, American educators have engaged in more self-criticism and more honest-to-goodness soul-searching than ever before in our history. This is all to the good. Let us hope and pray, however, that they will not panic or become hysterical under the stress of the current emergency. Let us hope and pray, in other words, that they will not decide to put all our educational eggs in the one basket of scientific and technological training—important as that kind of training obviously is and will continue to be for the indefinite future. That would be a tragic mistake. In the words of Pope Pius XII, a true education in this era of automation "must involve the whole man because in the advance of modern economy the qualities of a worker's character are of decisive importance.

"Furthermore, since particular aptitudes are required and modern workers must, at least within certain limits, be familiar with the whole process of production, with the branches of production and with the national economy, according to the different institutions created by modern labor legislation, it is necessary that vocational training and primarily the school give to them a sufficiently broad cultural background."

If we can develop this type of education for all our people —starting in the kindergarten or, better still, in the bosom of the family—there is every reason to hope that the emerging era of automation will be one of the greatest in the history of mankind.

THE BENEFITS AND PROBLEMS INCIDENT TO AUTOMATION AND OTHER TECHNOLOGICAL ADVANCES

ARTHUR J. GOLDBERG, *Chairman*

THREE central propositions have emerged in the Committee's consideration of the significance and impact of automation and other technological advances.

First, automation and technological progress are essential to the general welfare, the economic strength, and the defense of the nation.

Second, this progress can and must be achieved without the sacrifice of human values and without inequitable cost in terms of individual interests.

Third, the achievement of maximum technological development with adequate safeguards against economic injury to individuals depends upon a combination of private and governmental action, consonant with the principles of the free society.

Automation and technological change have meant much to our country. Today the average worker in the United States works shorter hours, turns out more goods, receives

241

higher wages, and has more energy harnessed and working with him than a worker anywhere else in the world. Increasingly, machines are relieving men of heavy physical labor and of dangerous and repetitive work. Competition in the world markets has been possible against foreign countries whose standards of living are below our own, though this advantage is diminishing. Finally, in a world split by ideological differences, automation and technological change have a tremendous and crucial role to play in maintaining the strength of the free world.

For these reasons, we emphasize at the outset the imperative need for and desirability of automation and technological change. Indeed, increased productivity and fuller utilization of resources are urgently needed to improve our rate of economic growth. They are likewise needed to improve our competitive position in world markets. Failure to advance technologically and to otherwise increase the productivity of our economy would bring on much more serious unemployment and related social problems than any we now face.

It is equally true that the current rate of technological advance has created social problems and that an acceleration of this rate may intensify these problems.

While advancing technology has given rise to new industries and jobs, it has also resulted in employee displacement; and the fact that new work opportunities are eventually created is no comfort or help to the displaced individual who cannot, for one reason or another, secure comparable or any employemnt. While employment has expanded in some industries, the net effect of rising output per worker, of the growing labor force and of other factors, has been an increase in the volume of unemployment during the past few years—even as total employment has reached new heights.

The impact of technology on agricultural employment has been particularly great. Along with other factors, it has resulted in over 1,600,000 workers—20 percent of the total —leaving the farms since 1950. Yet farm output has increased 28 percent, making available to our people an abundance of food, while there was famine in some of the communist countries. This increased output enabled this country to be of substantial assistance to needy people elsewhere in the world.

Our purpose, then, is to seek that course of action which will encourage essential progress in the form of automation and technological change, while meeting at the same time the social consequences such change creates.

We recognize that the subject of automation and technological change cannot be dealt with apart from two broader subjects: increased productivity in general, and unemployment.

We are preparing a separate report on Economic Growth, and only note here the basic importance of such growth to any consideration of the problems—and the opportunities—automation and technological advance present.

Regarding technological advance and unemployment, it is clear that unemployment has resulted from displacement due to automation and technological change. It is impossible, with presently available data, to isolate that portion of present unemployment resulting from these causes. Whether such displacement will be short-run depends to a considerable extent on our ability to anticipate and plan for programs involving technological change and to make better use of various mechanisms for retraining and relocating workers who find themselves unneeded in their former occupations. We have necessarily given general consideration in this Report to some aspects of the broader unemployment problem and to the prospects of more effective use of the work force.

A long stride toward solution of the unemployment problem will be made if we first recognize the nature of the problem. We regard the following factors as important in this connection:

(1) The recent rate of economic growth in the United States has been insufficient to reduce unemployment to a tolerable level.

(2) The exact extent of unemployment attributable to automation and technological change is unknown, since it is greatly complicated by other factors, such as:

a. The economic recession of 1960-61.

b. The unusually high entrance rate into the labor market, caused by the great post-war population increase. In the next ten years it is expected that there will be a net gain in the labor force of $13\frac{1}{2}$ million workers.

c. Chronic unemployment in distressed areas.

d. The effects of the rapid advances which have been made by foreign competitors.

e. Changing consumption patterns.

f. The changing nature of jobs which often leaves a gap between job requirements and qualifications of applicants. During the 1950's there was a 58 percent increase in the number of skilled technical and professional workers. Unskilled workers, with only a limited education, found it more difficult to get, or hold, a job. In this connection, the Department of Labor projections indicate that unless steps are taken to reduce the dropout rate among high school students, some $7\frac{1}{2}$ million of those new workers joining the labor force in the 1960's, or more than 30 percent, will not have completed high school, and over

2½ million of them will not even have completed grade school.

g. Discrimination against workers on the basis of age, sex, race and creed.

h. Multiple job holding by individuals.

i. The continuing movement of workers away from the farms.

(3) Public employment service facilities have been inadequate as well as seriously uneven in their effectiveness with respect to helping workers find new jobs, counseling them as to the kind of jobs which are liable to be available in the future and advising them as to job prospects in other geographical areas.

(4) The mobility of workers is reduced by factors running contrary to the demands of a dynamic society, and an economy in transition.

a. The non-transferability of pension, seniority and other accumulated rights may result in an employee's being dependent upon his attachment to a particular job as the sole means of protecting his equities.

b. Desirable and essential mobility is affected by reluctance to leave home—because of personal ties, or because other members of the family may be working; by the cost of moving and possible losses on local property; and by the insecurity of jobs in a new locality.

(5) Educational and informational facilities have been inadequate in that:

a. The requirements of general education prior to vocational and professional training have not kept pace with the shift in job opportunities.

b. The required types of vocational and technical training and retraining are often not available, e.g., for workers leaving the farm.

c. There has been an inadequate liaison among school systems, industry, and government with respect to future job requirements, and in fact there is insufficient information about the nature of such jobs.

d. There has been inadequate financial support for needy students.

e. Counseling facilities have been generally inadequate.

(6) Proper retraining facilities, and a system of financial support for workers while retraining, have been lacking.

These are some of the relevant circumstances of a society in which automation and technological advance are essential motive forces. The operation of these forces within the social context creates serious displacement problems—not as a necessary price of progress but as the stern consequence of failure to recognize and provide for these problems. We reject the too common assumption that continuing unemployment is an inherent cost of automation.

We believe, rather, that a combination of energetic and responsible private and public action will permit the advancement of automation and technological change without the sacrifice of human values, and that such combined efforts can cope satisfactorily with the total unemployment problem—including whatever part of it may arise from the displacements which result inevitably from the introduction of new devices and processes.

We do not attempt here an exhaustive exploration or enumeration of all the ways and means of achieving maximum technological progress with the minimum of individual disadvantage. Our suggestions can be only representative of a broader set of possibilities. We recognize, furthermore, that the totality of any combination of recommendations must be viewed in the light of such relevant factors as their costs to individual enterprises, their effect on the federal budget, and their influence on general price levels.

We recommend that serious consideration be given the following measures:

(1) Adoption by the government and others of policies which will promote a high rate of economic growth and fuller utilization of resources. A much higher rate of growth is essential and is the best device for reducing unemployment to tolerable levels. We will include in our forthcoming report on Economic Growth suggestions in this area.

(2) Acceptance by government agencies of the responsibility for collecting, collating, and disseminating information with respect to present and future job opportunities and requirements in a rapidly changing society.

(3) Cooperation between government and private organizations in the field of education in improving and supporting educational facilities to the end that:

    a. New entrants to the labor force will be better qualified to meet the occupational demands of the future;

    b. The dropout rate at grade and high school levels will be reduced;

    c. Better vocational, technical, and guidance programs will be available;

    d. Rural and depressed areas, where surplus workers reside, will be better served;

    e. Financial support will be available for deserving and needy students; and

    f. There will be a general up-grading in the quality of our education.

(4) Acceptance by management of responsibility for taking measures, to the maximum extent practicable, for lessening the impact of technological change, including:

247

a. Adequate lead time;

b. Open reporting to the employees involved;

c. Cooperation with representatives of the employees to meet the problem involved;

d. Cooperation with public employment services;

e. The timing of changes, to the extent possible, so that potential unemployment will be cushioned by expected expansion of operations and normal attrition in the work force (through separations resulting from retirement, quits, and so forth).

(5) Support from both public and private organizations for retraining of workers who have been and will be displaced.

a. Private employers and unions faced with automation or technological changes should make every reasonable effort to enable workers who are being displaced, and who need to be retrained, to qualify for new jobs available with the same employer, and to enjoy a means of support while so engaged.

b. Where it is not possible for the employer to reabsorb displaced workers, appropriately safeguarded public support in the form of subsistence payments should be available to industrial and agricultural workers who qualify for and engage in retraining.

c. Unemployment Compensation laws should be liberalized to permit and to encourage retraining.

(6) Support from both public and private sources, with due consideration to the circumstances of the enterprise involved, for the displaced worker who is seeking new employment.

a. The duration, coverage, and amount of unemployment compensation, where inadequate, should be increased and made subject to realistic uniform minimum requirements under the federal-state system.

b. Employer supplementation of public unemployment compensation should be accomplished through severance pay, supplemental unemployment benefits, and similar measures.

c. Attention should be given to provision for the special case of the worker who is displaced during the period when he is approaching retirement. This may appropriately include consideration of provision for early retirement, through private arrangements or social security measures; but alternative possibilities of more constructive temporary uses of such services warrant exploration.

(7) Support from both private and public sources to the end that a worker's job equities and security may be protected without impairment of his mobility. This will warrant consideration, taking into account relevant cost factors, of such measures as:

a. Financial aid in the transfer of employees to other plants in a multi-plant system, and protection of existing rights for individuals so transferred.

b. The use of public funds in order to give financial aid in the transfer of unemployed workers from one area to another where the result will be to provide continuing employment.

c. The improvement of public and private protection of pension rights.

d. The recognition by unions, individual employees, and employers of the necessity of adapting seniority and other rules in order to facilitate mobility of workers, while providing protection for the equities of employees.

The Committee notes particularly the need for further study and exploration of this vital area.

(8) Vast additional improvement of the public employment service so that it can effectively place, counsel, and re-

locate workers both locally and across state lines. We note with approval the start which has been made in this direction.

(9) Vigorous and unremitting efforts by all segments of the population—including government, employers, unions and employees—to eliminate discrimination in employment because of race, creed, age or sex.

(10) There are pressing national needs to be met, and an abundance of manpower available to meet these needs. This matching of manpower and national needs, which is part of the vital context of the automation and technological advance problem, will obviously be affected by various broader governmental policies. Reserving fuller consideration of this area for our Economic Growth report, we nevertheless note here that:

a. When technological changes or other factors develop particular pockets of unemployment, this becomes an additional reason for the undertaking, particularly at the state and local levels but with federal assistance where this is necessary, of public development projects for which there is need independent of the employment need itself.

b. Every effort should be made to maintain on an up-to-date and ready-to-go basis a schedule of needed public development projects, particularly those which could be started most quickly and which would be of short or controllable duration, so that the initiation of such projects can in the future be advanced, and the flow of projects already under way can be speeded up, if the manpower situation warrants this.

c. If the operation of the economy, including the effect of automation and technological change, creates or leaves an intolerable manpower surplus, consideration should be given to monetary and fiscal measures—including the possibility of appropriate tax re-

ductions—which would give promise of helping alleviate this situation.

d. Governmental action along the lines suggested here,
stimulated in part by the need to meet unemployment situations, would obviously have to take account of other considerations, including particularly
the maintenance of national economic stability and
security. We simply assert, however, the coordinate
importance of stability and growth.

(11) The need for goods and services must not be left unfilled, particularly in a time of international crisis. At
the same time, high unemployment is intolerable. In
the light of our current responsibilities to meet world
conditions, and in view of our unmet needs at home, we
consider the development of programs directed at the
achievement of full employment as being more significant at the present time than the consideration of a
general reduction in the hours of work. A reduction in
the basic work period has, however, historically been
one means of sharing the fruits of technological progress, and there may well develop in the future the
necessity and the desirability of shortening the work
period, either through collective bargaining or by law
or by both methods. In connection with such a development, consideration would necessarily be given to
which purchasing power could be maintained along
with a reduced work period.*

---

* Mr. Meany, Mr. Dubinsky, Mr. Harrison, Mr. Reuther, and Mr.
Keenan are of the view that this paragraph should read as follows: "The
need for goods and services must not be left unfilled, particularly in a
time of international crisis. At the same time, high unemployment is intolerable. In the light of our current responsibilities to meet world conditions, and in view of our unmet needs at home, we consider the development of programs directed at the achievement of maximum output
and full employment as most significant at the present time. However,
if unemployment is not reduced substantially in the near future we will
have to resort to a general shortening of the work period through col-

We affirm our conviction that the infinite promise of automation and technological advance can be realized without loss or cost of human values. America can enjoy the fruits of higher productivity without having to accept, as the inevitable result, serious social consequences growing out of the displacement of workers.

The recommendations made here suggest our view of a broader pattern of possible courses of action which would necessarily have to be adapted to particular circumstances, but which permit the constructive and responsible uses of technology and automation. We see no barriers—except misunderstanding, timidity and false fear—to the accomplishment of this purpose by a coordination of private and public programs wholly consonant with the essential concepts of the free society.

We assert the necessity of automation and technological development to the maintenance of American standards of living and to the fulfillment of this country's role of leadership in freedom's fight for survival. We assert equally the obligation and the capacity of Americans—as indi-

---

lective bargaining and by law. In connection with such a development, consideration would necessarily be given to the extent to which purchasing power could be maintained along with a reduced work period. A reduction in the basic work period has historically been one means of sharing fruits of technological progress."

Mr. McDonald, Mr. Reuther, and Mr. Keenan comment as follows: "We agree that, in the light of the considerations stated, the most desirable solution now to the problem of unemployment is the development of programs which will achieve full employment at forty hours per week. Saying that this is the most desirable solution is not, however, the same thing as saying that we have in fact achieved that solution or that we will in fact achieve it in the near future. And only the fact of full employment—not a statement of its desirability—can properly serve as the premise for the statement that the necessity for shortening the work period will only develop 'in the future.' If we fail, as we have so far failed, to achieve the most desirable solution we will have to move more quickly than we are now moving in the direction of shortening the work period."

viduals and as a group—to use these new instruments and methods to enrich the lives of *all* of us.

We see no reason for alarm if out of a greater sense of common purpose we can achieve the good will and the determination to act together.

January 11, 1962

Comments by Arthur F. Burns

on Report on

"The Benefits and Problems Incident to Automation and Other Technological Advances"

I FIND parts of this report highly constructive, particularly the recommendations designed (a) to achieve efficient and yet humane management of technological changes, (b) to improve the functioning of the labor market, and (c) to extend the coverage and otherwise strengthen the unemployment insurance system. Nevertheless, I am troubled by the report as a whole, and I consider it a dubious guide to economic policy.

The reasons for my dissent are as follows:

(1) The report fails to identify or to analyze or to assess the quantitative importance of the different causes of unemployment. Nevertheless, it conveys the impression that technological advances are a major, if not the major, cause of recent unemployment. I know of no evidence to support this view, and I deplore anything that adds to the greatly exaggerated fears that many people have of what is loosely called automation.

(2) The report suffers from a failure to link its proposed remedies to the causes of unemployment. Thus the report does not mention seasonal unemployment or ways

253

of dealing with it. It does not mention the loss of exports by some industries or the policies needed for coping with this source of unemployment. It does not distinguish cyclical unemployment from other types or indicate how public policy for dealing with recessions should be improved. On the other hand, the report puts heavy emphasis on public works and seems to suggest that this kind of governmental spending is a good remedy for unemployment regardless of its cause. Unhappily, public works are poorly suited for dealing with mild recessions or with local pockets of chronic unemployment.

(3) Most recommendations of the report are couched in such vague language that they may mean much or little, depending on how they are interpreted. But if experience is any guide, neither the vagueness of language nor the surrounding qualifications will prevent articulate groups of our society from claiming the authority of this committee for programs that could prove damaging to our economy. If all or most of the recommendations were implemented fairly promptly and on a liberal scale, both employer costs of production and governmental outlays would rise substantially. The report passes over lightly the question of how such increases would affect business profits or the Federal budget or the general price level. I find this question very troublesome at the present time. The deterioration of profit margins during the past decade is already a serious obstacle to achieving a high rate of economic growth. The protracted rise of the price level has already put severe pressure on our balance of international payments. This year's projected rise of Federal cash outlays already exceeds the increase of any peacetime year in our history and, the international situation being what it is, military expenditures may soon need to be still larger. In view of these facts, unless great caution

is exercised in pursuing programs that raise costs of
production or public outlays, we may find that economic growth is curbed, that confidence in the dollar
is weakened, and that our international political position is undermined.

(4) Apart from these dangers, the report fails to analyze
how its recommendations would affect the volume of
unemployment itself. The report seems to call not only
for liberalizing the unemployment insurance system,
but also for extending private supplements to unemployment insurance, for providing public subsistence
payments to workers who undergo retraining, for lower-
ing the age at which displaced workers can qualify for
social security, and for using public funds to aid unemployed workers in moving to areas where jobs can be
found. I deem it a duty to point out that if all these
measures were adopted in quick order and on a substantial scale, some individuals who now are outside
the labor force will see an advantage in entering it,
while there will be others who, having quit or lost their
jobs, will be tempted to take more time in settling on
new ones. In other words, unless great care and caution
are exercised in implementing the Committee's recommendations, the end result may well be the social mis-
fortune of permanently higher unemployment.

(5) In large part, the shortcomings of the report are traceable to the pessimistic assumption on which it seems to
proceed—namely, that there is a serious possibility that
our nation's economic progress will prove insufficient
to provide jobs for all those who are able and eager to
work. I have greater faith in our nation's future. A
tremendous expansion of prosperity lies within our
power. The degree to which we attain it will mainly
depend, first, on how much work people care to do,
second, on how productive they wish to be, third, on
how earnestly we pursue public policies to stimulate

255

new, creative, and more efficient economic activities by business enterprises. If the report had started from this broad but fundamental premise, it would have dealt more constructively with the economic and human problem of unemployment.

Comments by Henry Ford II

on Report on

"The Benefits and Problems Incident to Automation and Other Technological Advances"

I SHARE wholeheartedly the concern over unemployment expressed in this report, and I applaud this committee's desire both to speed industrial progress and to spread its human benefits more widely.

Few things are as costly to our nation, or as crushing to the human spirit, as lack of work for those who are willing and able to work.

Because I hold these views so strongly, I feel compelled to state my belief that this report does not really get to the heart of the matter.

Its major premise is the assumption that automation and technological advance are in and of themselves significant causes of unemployment—an assumption that neither history nor an analysis of current unemployment supports. Technological advance has been with us for many generations. But, popular beliefs to the contrary, technological advance has not been accelerating. Figures from the Bureau of Labor Statistics show, for recent years, an increase in productivity well below the average rate for the postwar period and not much different from the average rate since 1909.

Moreover, the factual evidence strongly indicates that,

while automation displaces some individuals from the jobs they have held, its over-all effect is to increase income and expand job opportunities. History teaches us that, by and large, workers displaced by technological advance have moved rapidly into other employment, ultimately to better-paying jobs. This is why we have had rising personal incomes rather than mass unemployment as new technology has come into use and productivity has increased.

As Solomon Fabricant has recently pointed out (in his introduction to John W. Kendrick's *Productivity Trends in the United States*):

Better-than-average increases in output were usually accompanied by better-than-average increases in employment of workers and tangible capital, despite the more rapid rise in productivity. Correspondingly, less-than-average increases in productivity were usually accompanied by less-than-average increases (or even decreases) in output and in the use of labor and capital resources. . . . No one concerned with the rise and fall of industries, or—to single out a currently discussed problem—with the effects of "automation" on employment, may ignore these basic facts.

When the economy is prosperous, displaced workers quickly find new employment. This is illustrated by the movement of workers off farms and into industrial employment when times are good, and the slowdown in this movement when times are bad.

The committee has recognized that the general problem of unemployment is the key problem, but its recommendations are concerned mainly with the important but secondary matters of retraining and mobility. A good employment service and unemployment compensation facilitate the transfer from one job to another, but these measures, even if accompanied by massive retraining, relief and other social programs, will scarcely make a dent in unemployment when economic conditions are poor.

If, therefore, we would help persons displaced by technological advance, we must focus our attention not on relief or even training—though these, properly conceived and administered, will help—but on creating new jobs for people who seek them and can perform in them.

When wages rise faster than productivity in the economy, costs will rise and then either prices will go up or profits will come down—or both will happen. If profits come down, then incentive to save and to invest savings in new, job-creating plants, enterprises and industries must suffer. Moreover, unless inflationary measures are taken to support the higher wage, cost and price levels, demand will not be adequate to maintain production and employment. And, when the integrity of the dollar is at stake, inflationary measures cannot be taken without calamitous results.

We must find ways consistent with a free economy to keep wages and other costs from causing either unemployment or inflation.

I regret that the report does not make this focal problem the primary target of its comments and recommendations. For, when we have found and placed in operation those policies and practices that can keep costs from rising and forcing us into either unemployment or inflation, we will have done much more than could be accomplished by all other measures combined.

The recommendations in this report are concerned mainly with ways of preventing and relieving technological displacement. I personally endorse many of them and the company with which I am associated has long followed practices similar to many of those recommended in the report.

Nevertheless, I have the following general reservations about the character of the recommendations:

First, they cannot solve the problem of mass unemployment because they are directed primarily at helping people to find jobs—not at the basic need for more jobs.

Second, the massive program of public and private actions called for may have unexpected consequences that the committee has not been able to evaluate. Indeed, I believe that the knowledge and experience necessary to evaluate this sweeping program do not now exist, and that it is, therefore, inappropriate and unwise for this committee to place its stamp of approval upon such a program. For example, greatly expanded Federal assistance could very well destroy incentives that stimulate private economic activity and generate individual initiative.

Third, the endorsement of comprehensive, economy-wide programs in very general terms diverts attention from and complicates the search for carefully selected measures to meet particular problems. For example, I believe that the main result of a large-scale, nationwide program to retrain the unemployed might be to impede the development of useful local programs carefully tailored to existing job opportunities and the needs and abilities of individuals.

In addition to these general reservations, I have misgivings about some of the specific recommendations.

With respect to unemployment compensation, I believe that duration, coverage and amount of benefits must be increased where they are inadequate. In addition, safeguards to protect against abuses should be strengthened. I do not endorse Federal standards, but believe the states should continue with responsibility for fitting their particular systems to their own conditions and needs.

I agree that in the main the recommendations for improving our school systems are good. In many areas and localities, however, the most urgent need is not more money but greater public concern with what is taught in our schools.

Arbitrarily shortening the workweek in order to decrease unemployment would be a confession of defeat. Not only a poor remedy, it is also a harmful one; for it would retard the growth needed for the safety and welfare of our nation at this point in its history. We can and should look forward to normal increases in our leisure time, but they must come as our growing economy can afford them and not as expedient solutions to unemployment problems.

In summary, I find some things in this report of which I approve, and much of which I disapprove. Its goal of making certain that high employment accompany technological improvement and increasing efficiency has my full support. However, I believe that the general direction of its recommendations is not well-calculated to achieve this goal. I believe, too, that the report's basic assumption concerning the relationship between technological advance and unemployment is in error.

Therefore, I feel it necessary to say, with reluctance, that I cannot concur in the report of the President's Committee.

A SELECTED BIBLIOGRAPHY
ON AUTOMATION

1. Abruzzi, A., "Automation, Work and Work Morality," *Panel Symposium on Automation*. Atlanta, Georgia: American Association for the Advancement of Science, December 27, 1955.

2. American Management Association, *Keeping Pace with Automation, Practical Guides for the Company Executive,* Special Report No. 7. New York, 1955.

3. *Automation Bibliography (Selected)*. Washington, D. C.: Government Printing Office, Federal Mediation and Conciliation Service, September, 1955. 7 pp.

4. *Automation Dictionary*. Philadelphia: Minneapolis-Honeywell Regulator Co., 1955.

5. *The Automation Factory—What Does It Mean?* Report on the conference held at Margate, June 16th-19th, 1955. London: The Institution of Production Engineers. 217 pp. A Collection of twenty-one papers dealing with many phases of the automatic factory, machines and implications of automation.

261

6. *Automation—Engineering for Tomorrow.* General Sessions Addresses from the Centennial Symposium of the School of Engineering, Michigan State University, East Lansing, Michigan, May 13, 1955.

7. Bailey, Sidney, *Automation in North America.* A report on visits to industrial, commercial and research establishments in U. S. and Canada. London: H. M. Stationery Office, 1958.

8. Barkin, Davis, Saurino, Whyte, eds., *Industrial Productivity.* Madison, Wisconsin: Industrial Relations Research Association, 1951. A collection of articles on economic and social effects of automation and technological change.

9. Bendiner, Robert, "Age of the Thinking Robot and What It Will Mean to Us," *The Reporter,* April 7, 1955.

10. *Bibliography of Automation: A List of Selected Readings for High Schools.* Urbana, Illinois: University of Illinois, Institute of Labor and Industrial Relations, 1956. 13 pp.

11. *Bibliography on the Use of IBM Machines in Science, Statistics and Education.* New York: International Business Machines Corporation, January, 1956. 907 Listings. 81 pp.

12. Bittel, Lester R., Practical Automation, *Methods for Increasing Plant Productivity.* New York: McGraw-Hill, 1957.

13. Booth, Andrew D., *Automation and Computing.* New York: Macmillan, 1958.

14. Bright, James R., Automation and Management. Boston: Division of Research, Graduate School of Business Administration, Harvard University, 1958.

15. Brozen, Y., "The Economics of Automation," *American Economic Review.* Papers and Proceedings of the 69th

Annual Meeting of the American Economic Association, December 27th-29th, 1956. May, 1957. 339-350.

16. Buckingham, Walter S., *Automation: Its Impact on Business and People.* New York: Harper, 1961.

17. *The Challenge of Automation.* Papers delivered at the National Conference on Automation. Washington, D. C.: Public Affairs Press, 1958. 77 pp.

18. Cheek, Gloria, *Economic and Social Implications of Automation: A Bibliography Review.* East Lansing, Michigan: Labor and Industrial Relations Center, Michigan State University, 1960.

19. Cleator, Philip E., *The Robot Era.* New York: Thomas Y. Growell, 1955.

20. *Conference on Automation Control. Proceedings.* 1951. Granfeld, England: Butterworth's Scientific Publications, Academic Press, 1952. 584 pp.

21. Congress of Industrial Organizations, Committee on Economic Policy. *The Challenge of Automation.* Papers delivered by Joseph C. O'Mahoney and others at the National Conference of Automation. Washington, D. C.: Public Affairs Press, 1955.

22. Diebold, John, *Automation: The Advent of the Automatic Factory.* Princeton, New Jersey: D. Van Nostrand Co., 1952.

23. Diebold, John, *Automation: Its Impact on Business and Labor,* and a statement by the National Planning Association Committee on Automation, Planning Pamphlet No. 106. Washington, D. C.: National Planning Association, 1959.

24. Dreher, Carl, *Automation, What It Is, How It Works, Who Can Use It.* New York: W. W. Norton, 1957.

25. Drucker, P. F., *America's Next Twenty Years.* New York: Harper Brothers, 1955.

26. Einzig, Paul, *The Economic Consequences of Automation.* London: Secker and Warburg, 1956.

27. Friedmann, George, *Industrial Society, The Emergence of the Human Problems of Automation.* Glencoe, Ill.: The Free Press, 1955.

28. George, F., *Automation, Cybernetics and Society.* New York: The Philosophical Library, 1959.

29. Giulbaud, G. T., *What Is Cybernetics?* New York: Criterion Books, 1959.

30. Grabbe, Eugene M., *Automation in Business and Industry.* New York: John Wiley and Sons, 1958.

31. Grabbe, Eugene M., *Handbook of Automation, Computation and Control.* New York: John Wiley and Sons, 1958.

32. Griscom, Clement A., *Automation and the Women Workers.* Philadelphia: University of Pennsylvania, 1956.

33. Hawley, George F., *Automating the Manufacturing Process.* New York: Reinhold Publishing Co., 1959.

34. Hugh-Jones, Edward M., ed., *The Push-Button World: Automation Today.* Norman, Oklahoma: University of Oklahoma Press, 1956.

35. *Instrumentation and Automation.* Hearings before the Joint Committee on the Economic Report. Eighty-fourth Congress, December 12th-14th, 1956. Washington, D. C.: U. S. Government Printing Office, 1957. 201 pp.

36. Leaver, E. W., "How Automatic Can We Get? An Over-All View," *Keeping Peace With Automation, Practical Guides for the Company Executive, Special Report No. 7.* New York: American Management Association, 1955. 136 pp.

37. Levin, Howard S., *Office Work and Automation.* New York: John Wiley and Sons, 1955.

38. Lilley, Samuel, *Automation and Social Progress.* London: Lawrence and Wishart, 1957.

39. Michael, Donald N., *Cybernation: The Silent Conquest.* Santa Barbara, California: Center for the Study of Democratic Institutions, 1962. 48 pp.

40. *Man and Automation.* Report on the Proceedings of a Conference sponsored by the Society for Applied Anthropology at Yale University, December 27th-28th, 1955. New Haven, Conn.: The Technology Project, Yale University, 1956. 117 pp.

41. Osborn, P. G., *Automation of Industry—A Geographical Consideration.* Chicago: Department of Geography, University of Chicago, September, 1953.

42. Pieper, Josef, *Leisure, the Basis of Culture.* New York: Pantheon, 1960.

43. Pollock, Frederick, *Automation: A Study of Its Economic and Social Consequences.* New York: Praeger, 1957.

44. Pyke, Magnus, *Automation: Its Purpose and Future.* New York: The Philosophical Library, 1957.

45. Ross, K. F. X., *Automation, Servant of Man.* New York: Lothrop, Lee and Shepherd, 1958.

46. Rusinoff, Samuel Eugene, *Automation in Practice.* Chicago: American Technical Society, 1957.

47. Shultz, George P., *Automation, A New Dimension to Old Problems.* Washington, D. C.: Public Affairs Press, 1955.

48. Soule, George H., *Time for Living.* New York: The Viking Press, 1955.

49. U. S. Bureau of Labor Statistics, *Automatic Technology and Its Implications.* A selected annotated bibliography prepared by Edgar Weinberg. Washington, D. C.: U. S. Government Printing Office, 1956.

50. U. S. Congress Joint Committee on the Economic Report, *Automation and Technological Change.* Hearings before the Subcommittee on Economic Stabilization of the Joint Committee of the Economic Report. Eighty-fourth Congress of the U. S. Washington, D. C.: U. S. Government Printing Office, 1955.

INDEX

Administration, 80, 81
Advance notice, 57, 78
Adversary system, 129, 140
AFL-CIO, 24, 26
AFL Building Trades, 23
Amalgamated Meat Cutters Union, 79, 216
American Telephone and Telegraph Co., 79, 95
Area Redevelopment Administration (ARA), 74, 75
Armour and Co., 79
Automation, affecting blue collar workers, 3, 30, 123; affecting white collar workers, 3, 30, 91, 123; cybernetics, 8, 10, 264; defined, 7 ff., 70, 88, 128; ethical questions, 3, 11, 37, 65, 68, 73, 76, 77, 104, 107, 108, 217; human aspects, 14, 16, 45, 53, 54, 59, 63, 65, 66, 80, 106, 107, 110, 120, 131, 145, 197, 200, 218; problems associated with, 3, 12, 17, 22, 49, 51, 54, 55, 67, 76, 77, 88, 104, 107, 114

Barkin, Solomon, 21, 262
Bennett, John C., 146, 149
Berle, Adolf, 95, 97
Blue collar workers, 3, 30, 123
Boredom, 72, 217
Brennan, Niall, 14
Brotherhood of Railway Clerks, 235
Buckingham, Walter, 71, 112n., 261, 263
Burns, Arthur F., 253 ff.

Capitalism, 97, 222; competitive concept of, 25

Carey, James B., 216
Chamber of Commerce, 65, 82
Chronic unemployment, 60, 65-85
CIO industrial unions, 23
Clark, Senator Joseph S., 81, 93, 94
Coal mining, 22, 217; regions, 70
Cold war, 12, 25, 26
Collective bargaining, 19, 20, 21, 22, 25, 37, 38, 39, 55, 57, 58, 62, 78, 122, 124, 140, 226, 251, 252n.
Common good, 15, 21, 25
Communism, 97, 146, 197
Compensation, unemployment, 221, 223, 224, 225, 248, 257, 259; see Supplemental unemployment benefits
Computer technology, 9, 10, 104, 105
Continental Copper and Steel Industries, 90
Contracts, 13, 75, 96, 187, 226
Cybernetics, 8, 10, 264

Dankert, Clyde, E., 214
Depreciation allowances, 74, 189
Depressed areas, 65, 68, 70, 74, 75, 76, 85, 222
Detroit, 69, 70
Diebold, John, 263
Discrimination, 69, 78, 100, 245, 250
Displaced workers, 22, 54, 61, 62, 69, 73, 78, 122, 136, 148, 221, 242, 248, 257
Displacement, 14, 71, 73, 243, 246, 257
Dropouts, 32, 33, 67, 244, 247
Drucker, Peter, 214, 264
Duties, see Obligations

Economic policies, 58 f.; productivity, 11, 15, 16, 25, 69, 70, 124, 220, 223, 242, 243, 247, 252

Education, 32-36, 59, 61, 69, 77, 136, 194, 209, 210, 212, 239, 240, 244, 245, 247; vocational training, 66, 71, 191, 245, 247

Eisenhower, President, 23, 24

Employment, 12, 59, 61, 79, 89, 91, 114, 215, 217

Employment Act of 1946, 58

Ethical questions arising from automation, see Automation

Evolution, 179, 182, 208

Fabricant, Solomon, 257

Farm program, 94, 215

Federal government, 20, 75, 77, 78, 125, 248, 250; see Government

Federal Trade Commission, 95

Ford II, Henry, 44, 256 ff.

Ford Motor Co., 24, 44

Fortune magazine, 4, 21, 223

Fund for the Republic, 20, 265

General Motors, 24, 95

Goldberg, Secretary Arthur J., 19, 21, 23, 24, 50, 81, 241

Goldwater, Senator Barry M., 74, 187

Government aid, 13, 79, 250, 251, 254, 259; see Federal government

Government assumption of responsibility, 50, 62, 206, 207, 220, 222, 237, 238, 241, 247; see Federal government

Gross national product, 31, 74

Guaranteed annual wage, 3, 44, 55

Harrison, George, 235, 236, 251n.

Health, 43, 59, 61, 122, 223, 224

Holland, Congressman Elmer J., 123

Housing, public, 59, 136

Human dimension, 14, 16, 45, 53, 54, 59, 63, 65, 66, 80, 106, 107, 110, 120, 131, 145, 197, 200, 218

Industrial society, relation to human nature, 15

Intellectual apostolate, 166; deterioration, 72, 203, 205

International Association of Electrical and Machine Workers, 216

International Brotherhood of Electrical Workers, 56, 118, 119, 120, 121

International Longshoremen's and Warehousemen's Union, 79

John XXIII, see Popes

Joint Economic Committee of Congress, 71, 84n.

Judaeo-Christian tradition, 66

Justice, 227; elemental, 40; social, 54

Keenan, Joseph D., 113, 251n., 252n.

Kennedy, President John F., 25, 26, 74, 135, 136, 189; Senator, 66

Kolko, Gabriel, 93

Labor and Management, 19 ff., 58, 69

Labor force, increase, 28, 50, 67; age distribution of, 29

Labor-Management Advisory Committee, 25, 26

Labor's viewpoint, 12 ff., 49-63, 113

Lamb, James J., 234, 235

Leisure, 3, 5, 72, 101, 199-212, 239, 260; education for, 209 ff., 212; serious and pastime, 204, 205

Leo XIII, see Popes

Lewis, John L., 221

McCarthy, Senator Eugene J., 66, 70, 75, 99, 213

McDonald, David, 216, 252n.

McNamara Committee, 98

Machlup, Fritz, 76

Machinists, 23

Making of a Moron, 14

Management's viewpoint, 10 ff., 78, 103, 127

Management Principles of Automation, 121

Manpower Development and Training Act of 1961, 81

Marx, Karl, 97, 220

Marxists, 222

Mater et Magistra, 53, 153, 166, 218, 220

Meany, George, 24, 251

Mechanization, distinction between automation and, 72
Mill, John Stuart, 220
Moonlighting, 62, 201, 245

Nadal, S.J., Jerome, 155, 158, 159
National Association of Manufacturers, 17, 23, 24, 25, 26, 92
Natural resources, preservation and development of, 59, 61
Negro, 34, 69, 77
Nixon, Richard, 23
Northeastern Pennsylvania Industrial Development Commission, 75

Obligation, 4, 37, 40, 77, 78, 107, 110, 126, 191, 193, 219, 220, 226, 238, 247, 253; ethical, 73, 148; moral, 76, 77, 83, 219; social, 37, 76
Older workers, 3, 14, 34, 66, 67, 70, 87-102, 235
Opus Dei, 166, 167, 171, 173
Ownership, 235 ff.; see Property

Pacific Maritime Association, 79
Pension agreements, 42, 97, 249
Pensions, 57, 62, 100
Pius XI, see Popes
Pius XII, see Popes
Polanco, S.J., Juan, 156
Popes, 131; John XXIII, 53, 125, 166, 218, 220, 227; Leo XIII, 25, 39, 40, 125; Pius XI, 25, 125; Pius XII, 15, 16, 132, 164, 168, 169, 170, 231, 232, 233, 234, 237, 240
Population, increase, 27, 244; shift, 95
Pratt and Whitney, 92
Productivity, sharing fruits of, 54, 60
Productivity Trends in the United States, 257
Profit, 133, 135; sharing, 223
Property, 97 ff.; see Ownership

Quadragesimo Anno, 15

Railroad Brotherhoods, 23; industry, 221

Recessions, 50, 51, 96, 244
Recommendations, 13, 61, 99, 247
Reconstruction Finance Corporation (RFC), 75
Redevelopment, metropolitan, 59, 61
Relocation, 14, 70, 76, 77, 80, 81, 82, 122; subsidies, 59
Rerum Novarum, 15, 39, 40
Responsibilities, see Obligations
Retirement, 14, 62, 122
Retraining, 14, 22, 58, 66, 70, 76, 77, 80, 81, 82, 100, 120, 121, 122, 124, 148, 222, 235, 245, 248, 258
Retraining programs, 58, 71
Reuther, Walter, 23, 24, 251n., 252n.
Right of association, 37, 38
Right to organize, 37, 38
Right-to-work laws, 23
Rights and obligations, 4, 37, 40

St. Francis Xavier, 164
St. Ignatius Loyola, 155, 157, 158, 159, 160
Selekman, Benjamin M., 78
Senate Committee on Unemployment Problems, 66, 70, 83n., 99, 214
Senate Labor and Public Welfare Committee, 191, 226
Seniority, 54, 56, 97, 122
Severance pay, 100, 122, 236, 249
Sherman and Clayton Acts, 95
Silent firing, 73
Slichter, Sumner, 214
Slum clearance, 59, 98
Social necessity, 98
Social order, 15, 16
Social security, guarantees, 59; Security, 59, 97, 224; retirement age, 62
Socialism, 46
Spiritual Exercises, 160
Standard of living, 11
Subcommittee on Employment and Manpower (Senate Committee on Labor and Public Welfare), 81
Subsidiarity, 15, 16
Suhard, Emmanuel Cardinal, 164
Supplemental unemployment bene-

fits, 44, 45, 65, 97, 100, 122, 221, 223, 236, 249
Supreme Court, 78

Tax benefits, 74; measures, 58, 62, 74, 76, 78, 250
Teamsters, 23, 49
Technological evolution, 8, 10, 12
Teilhard de Chardin, 176-179
Theological Conceptions of Goals for Economic Life, 146
Training, 57, 58, 66, 70, 219, 235

Unemployment, 63, 65-85, 89, 92, 96, 114, 123, 243, 244 ff.; class and mass, 66, 83; compensation, 76, 97
Union, role of, 52 ff.
United Auto Workers, 23, 44, 226
United Mine Workers, 221
United Packinghouse Workers, 79

United States Employment Service, 61, 62, 79
United States Steel Co., 193
United Steelworkers of America, 89, 216
Unskilled workers, 34, 66, 70, 71, 244

Wage supports, 58
Wages, 4, 11, 12, 13, 26, 40, 41, 55, 133, 149, 187, 194, 214, 237, 242; proper, 39
Welfare provision, 43, 122
West Coast Longshoremen's Agreement, 56
White collar workers, 3, 30, 91, 123
Wiener, Dr. Norbert, 107, 112
Women, 30, 66, 68, 73, 76, 219
Work force, 27, 29, 35, 50, 68

Youth, 27, 28, 66, 77, 80

A NOTE ON THE TYPE

IN WHICH THIS BOOK IS SET

This book is set in Baskerville, a Linotype face, created from the original types used by John Baskerville, the eighteenth-century typefounder and printer. This type has long been considered one of the finest book types ever developed. The letters are wide and open and have a businesslike approach. The finer hairlines give exquisite delicacy. The heavier strokes give color and strength. The relation of the two in combination gives a brilliant effect and makes for easy reading. The book was composed and printed by the Wickersham Printing Company of Lancaster, Pa., and bound by Moore and Company of Baltimore. The typography and design are by Howard N. King.